Please renew/return this item by the last date shown.

So that your telephone call is charged at local rate, please call the numbers as set out below:

	From Area codes 01923 or 0208:	From the rest of Herts:
Renewals:	01923 471373	01438 737373
Enquiries:	01923 471333	01438 737333
Minicom:	01923 471599	01438 737599

L32b

Hertfordshire
COUNTY COUNCIL
Community Information

2 6 JAN 2002

6/1/11
7/12

L32a

D1433177

Portsmouth: *a history*

Portsmouth: *a history*

A. TEMPLE PATTERSON
Emeritus Professor in the University of Southampton

 *Moonraker Press*

© 1976 A. Temple Patterson
First published in 1976 by
MOONRAKER PRESS
26 St Margarets Street, Bradford-on-Avon, Wiltshire
SBN 239 00146 X
Text set in 10/11 pt Monotype Plantin, printed by letterpress, and bound
in Great Britain at The Pitman Press, Bath

Contents

List of Illustrations

Preface and Acknowledgements

The present seems to me a timely moment for a new and (despite its deficiencies and limitations) a down-to-date history of Portsmouth to be written. For Portsmouth is a city on the march, revivified in a new shape after the devastating blows it suffered in the second world war, followed so soon afterwards by the drastic changes and reduction of the Navy. After these it might have become, as some indeed thought it would become, a city living on its memories of the past. Instead it is experiencing a striking metamorphosis. Its delicate and complex relationship with our diminished but modernised Navy still survives, though it no longer dominates the city's life. More important perhaps, and certainly more dramatic, are the reconstruction and development, alike of industry and commerce and of the physical face of the city, through which it is breaking out of the mould in which history had set it— that of a great naval base and little more—while retaining all of its historical interest and significance. The fact that the appearance of this book coincides approximately with a notable change in our system of local government may also add a little to its appropriateness.

For the provision of some of the material for the most modern section of the book I am much indebted to Mr J. R. Haslegrave the Chief Executive of Portsmouth. At a number of points I have leant heavily for source-material on several contributors to the series of monographs on local history entitled *The Portsmouth Papers*, of which I am the general editor, and notably on Miss Dorothy Dymond, Professor Barry Cunliffe, Mr John Webb, Mrs M. J. Hoad, Mr H. Sargeant, Mr Alistair Geddes, Dr R. C. Riley and Dr Edwin Course, all of whom I hope will accept this expression of my warmest appreciation and gratitude. For leave to reproduce illustrations and aid in obtaining them I owe thanks to the Keeper of H.M. the Queen's Pictures, the National Maritime Museum, the Portsmouth City Museums and City Libraries, the City Engineer's Reprographic Department, the former City Archivist Mr M. J. W. Willis-Fear, Mr Burton and Mr A Corney of the City Museums, Mrs M. J. Guy and her colleagues of the City Reference Library, Alderman F. A. J. Emery-Wallis and the late Mr S. G. Kerry.

The author and publisher gratefully acknowledge the assistance of the City of Portsmouth and the University of Southampton in the publication of this book.

1. The first 'Old Portsmouth': Portchester

Portsmouth is a city that has been shaped for good or ill by geography and history; first for good and afterwards partly for ill. The waters that made it our greatest naval base and for a long time the world's lie at the centre of England's southern coast and are sheltered by the Isle of Wight from almost any violent winds. These waters are firstly the Solent, which includes the Spithead* roadstead, a safe and spacious anchorage for hundreds of ships; and then the large natural harbours of the Hampshire coast, splayed out like the fingers of a hand of which Southampton Water may be considered the elongated thumb and Portsmouth Harbour the forefinger. Most of the Solent and Spithead is deep water and much of it is firm holding ground where ships can ride at anchor safe from dragging. But nature has done less for the wide landlocked harbours and the estuaries which form the rest of these waters, for only persistent dredging has enabled Portsmouth and Southampton to meet the needs of modern ships, while Langstone and Chichester Harbours to the eastward are still great sheets of shallow water at high tide and stretches of mud when the tide is out. Thanks to this dredging, however, Portsmouth Harbour, which is large enough to have held the whole British Fleet even at its maximum strength, has always had sufficient water even at low tide. Its entrance is not encumbered by any shallow bars or shoals, and its narrowness intensifies the scouring effect of the seven hours' flow and five hours' ebb of the tidal stream. Outside it the water runs out south-eastward at an angle, leaving a deep channel close to the shore, while the mud and sand it throws south-westward have formed the Spit Bank, which protects the harbour mouth from heavy seas driven by the south-westerly gales. Moreover the Spit and the other shoals further out (Horse Sand, Nomansland and the Motherbank) have helped by breaking the force of the seas on almost all sides of Spithead to make it the splendid

---

* Spithead, strictly defined, extends for two miles from south-east to north-west along the south-west side of the Spit Sand (mentioned above) with an average breadth of a mile and a half.

anchorage that it is. And when in the Middle Ages cross-Channel expeditions and naval warfare began to develop, Portsmouth's conveniently central position on the south coast, well placed for the junction of naval forces from east and west and facing the estuary of the Seine that formed the waterway first into friendly Normandy and later into hostile France, was bound to bring it to the fore.

Some of these advantages were shared by Southampton, and there has been more than one moment in history when it might have developed as a naval base as well as Portsmouth, or even instead of it. But their very different hinterlands have long pointed them towards their different destinies. Southampton, in the days when inland traffic was conducted more by waterways than overland, commanded routes to and from the interior of southern England by way of its two converging rivers, the Test and the Itchen; and its double high tide, producing long periods of relatively high water, made it easier for the trading ships of these early centuries to unload their cargoes. By contrast Portsmouth's magnificent or potentially magnificent harbour has no inflowing river; it lies shut in (or protected, as Palmerston and his mid-Victorian military and naval advisers saw) on the landward side by the long range of Portsdown Hill. Hence it has been a snug and secure place—always provided that there is command of Spithead—for a fighting fleet and its appurtenances, supplies and in due course its dockyard.

But with the mention of the dockyard we come not only to the great *raison d'être* of its growth but paradoxically enough to the first of the two disadvantages it has suffered in modern times and from which it is only now breaking free. The development of the dockyard has meant not only that it has tended to thrive in war but decline in peace (though this point must not be pushed too far) but also that it has been a town with all its eggs in one basket. Till very recently it had relatively little other industry or trade and therefore was so hard hit by the modern shrinkage of our navy that it was talked of as a dying city—a gloomy forecast which it is now in the process of disproving. Moreover since dockyard wages were never very high Portsmouth's dependence on it brought about a low-wage economy.

And here we come to the other difficulty from which it is bursting free. The first has been imposed in modern times by its history, but this one by its geography. It grew up on an island, linked to the mainland only by a single road-bridge until the railway appeared in the nineteenth century and then a second road-bridge well on in the twentieth. When therefore it had expanded until it covered practically the whole of this island by about 1900 it found itself hampered or checked in its further expansion by problems of transport and communication.

The solutions to these two difficulties, however, are bound up very closely together. In the last twenty years the city has set to work with considerable success to attract new and varied industries. But to find land for these and to house the workers in them it has had largely to go to the mainland. Only by thus turning towards the mainland can it have the future it seeks. And that has meant an escalation of its traffic and transport problems with which it is now grappling.

The first 'Old Portsmouth', however, was not even on Portsea Island at all. It was at the head of the harbour, on a tongue of land jutting out into it from the north, that a naval base originally arose. This earliest 'Old Portsmouth' was Portchester, the site of a prehistoric settlement and later a Roman fort. The first traces of occupation which have been found on this promontory date from the second half of the first century A.D., but even after the excavations recently conducted by the brilliant and distinguished Portsmouth-born archaeologist Professor Barry Cunliffe, there is little as yet to suggest the nature of this primitive settlement, since all that survives is a modest amount of pottery and a few stake-holes and post-holes suggesting small-scale peasant occupation like that found elsewhere on the fringes of the neighbouring harbours. During the second and third centuries A.D. the level of the sea seems to have risen, apparently driving the local inhabitants to retreat gradually to drier land further inland. But the slight hillock on which Portchester stands would have remained firm and dry, and thus caught the eyes of Roman military surveyors exploring the south and east coasts of the province of Britain for sites for what have come to be rather romantically called the Forts of the Saxon Shore.

There had been a Roman fleet based on Britain since the invasion in 43 A.D. which led to its occupation, and by the second century naval detachments were stationed at several harbours along the Channel coast from Dover to Pevensey, while there were similar bases on the neighbouring shore of Gaul. Early in the third century the raids across the North Sea of pirates from Germany apparently caused this system to be extended northwards to the coasts of Kent and Norfolk. Then after civil strife within the Roman Empire in the 270s the defences deteriorated and the pirates broke through the Straits of Dover and began to raid the lands on both sides of the Channel. The command of the fleet in Britain and with it the task of clearing and keeping the narrow seas were entrusted to a certain Carausius, himself a native of the Low Countries, whose massive bullnecked head on the coins he later struck suggests a resolute but unscrupulous character. Although he succeeded immediately in capturing scores of pirate ships and seizing their accumulated plunder, he neither restored this to its rightful owners nor sent it to the imperial treasury but kept nearly the whole of it for himself. This caused the Emperor Maximian presently to conclude that he was allowing the pirates a free hand till they were laden with spoil and only then descending upon them, wherefore he ordered his arrest and execution. Carausius's answer was to proclaim himself Emperor of Britain and set up in 286 an independent government which at least had the merit of efficiency. For seven years he maintained himself, until he fell, not to the forces of the legitimate emperors*, but to the dagger of his own treacherous lieutenant Allectus. Three years later Allectus was defeated and slain by one of the rightful monarchs and Britain was restored to its allegiance to Rome.

It is generally assumed that it was to cope with these pirate raids on the Channel coast that the great Roman fort at Portchester—the only one in northern Europe whose *enceinte* still stands intact—was built, along with several others. Enclosing an area of nine acres, its walls were ten feet thick and originally twenty or more in height, with a series of regularly-spaced D-shaped bastions projecting from them on which the giant catapults called *ballistae* could be mounted to provide both forward and flanking fire. Such bastions were a notable feature of late third-century Roman military architecture, and it is thought that Portchester and the other contemporary forts must have been the first examples of this new style to appear in Britain, apart from some town gates. The evidence of coins found there during excavations shows that the fort was probably built at some time after 268, and Professor Cunliffe considers it a reasonable supposition that it was built by Carausius. Whether in that event he built it against the pirates before his revolt or afterwards against the threat of reconquest by the legitimate Roman rulers is uncertain. Professor Cunliffe inclines to the former alternative, but (to quote him) 'if so, who is to say what was in his mind when he began to build?'[1]

After the defeat and death of Allectus, Portchester, like several of the other forts, shows signs of abandonment or at least a drastic reduction in garrison and does not seem to have been reoccupied on a large scale till about 340. A reduction of the garrison would have fitted in well with the politics of the times, for Allectus's conqueror Constantius Clorus (the father of Constantine the Great), having presumably realised the strength of the coastal forts during the rebellion, would very possibly have reduced their garrisons in case another usurper might make use of them. This incidentally suggests that the seas were now swept clear of pirates. The conditions revealed by excavation as prevailing in the fort around 300 and after, however—a state of overcrowding and squalor such as surely no commander would have tolerated, with rubbish piled up against the walls—suggests rather that it may have been full of squatters or refugees, or even have been used as a kind of concentration camp for some of the survivors of Allectus's party and their dependents. Then at some time in the late 330s or the 340s the forts seem to have been reorganised (perhaps the pirates had become troublesome again) and it may have been the Emperor Con-

---

* Because of the size of the Empire it was now divided between two (and later four) emperors.

stans, who visited Britain in 342, who was responsible for this. At Portchester the archaeological evidence shows that about this time the roadways within the fortress were remetalled and there are some traces of timber buildings. An interesting feature of this period is the presence of women within the fort, attested by the discovery of bracelets, brooches, hairpins and the signs of several burials of immature infants. This implies that the garrison was now a peasant militia who had their families with them, a practice well known on other parts of the frontier of the Empire after 370, though at Portchester it must be earlier. The primary function of the garrison would then have been to act as a kind of marine commando unit prepared to embark in ships and drive off pirates when they were sighted or go by land to any point where a raiding-party might have come ashore.

About 370 came the end of the military occupation of the site. Three years earlier barbarian hordes of Picts, Scots, Saxons and Franks had combined to attack the Roman province of Britain from three sides at once and had overrun it as far south as the Thames. In 368 Theodosius, a distinguished soldier, had been sent with a large force to save the situation and had gradually managed to restore temporary peace and stability by a combination of buying off the invaders and reorganising the coastal defences. But whereas most of the coastal forts show clear signs of this reorganisation there are none at Portchester. Indeed the coin series there ends abruptly about 370, implying that military occupation had ceased. On the other hand a marked strengthening of the defences of Clausentum, the Romano-British port near the mouth of the Itchen which may be reckoned the first Southampton, took place at this time. Professor Cunliffe's tentative conclusion is therefore that the latter was then substituted for Portchester as a coastal fortress, perhaps because difficulty had been experienced in sailing out of Portsmouth Harbour at certain tides.

What happened to the site in the remaining forty years or so of the Roman era is obscure, but it is very unlikely that it was ever completely abandoned. The barracks and other old timber buildings which had previously existed within the walls and of which traces have been found would have offered some protection to would-be inhabitants, and the finding of a coin of the Emperor Arcadius (395–408) shows that the site was still in use or visited in the early fifth century. It is true that no trace of buildings belonging to this period has yet been found, but in 1966 evidence came to light which Professor Cunliffe considers can safely be dated to the fifth or sixth centuries, suggesting that the area within the fort had been ploughed.

After the Roman legions and fleets left Britain in the early fifth century the history of the region that the conquering English afterwards called *Hamtunscire* or Hampshire, and indeed of the whole country, becomes a matter of conjecture and controversy. The conquest and settlement of Hampshire by the English are wrapped in obscurity and bedevilled by dispute, though archaeology and the study of place-names have done something to supplement and clarify the scanty, puzzling and sometimes even contradictory scraps of written evidence. The tribal or racial identity, places of origin, direction of approach, points of entry and area of first settlement of those 'English' war-bands who soon seized upon this part of the land are still matters of debate into which it is perhaps hardly necessary to enter here. To 501, however, is ascribed an outstanding example of these perplexing or dubious pieces of written evidence, namely the much-discussed entry in the Anglo-Saxon Chronicle (compiled in the later ninth century but incorporating earlier material) which states that

Port and his two sons Bieda and Maegla came to Britain with two ships in the place which is called Portes mutha, and killed a young British man, a very noble man.

Since according to the balance of opinion Portchester was known in Roman times as Portus Adurni and there is no need to look further for the origin of the name Portsmouth—'the mouth of the port'—this annal has often been dismissed as a fabrication and a notorious example of eponymism. Sir John Myres, for example, wrote that it 'could only be saved from condemnation as an antiquarian invention by invoking a coincidence stranger than fiction';[2] though on the other hand Sir Frank Stenton showed an inclination to invoke just such a coincidence by pointing out that this view did not explain the appearance of the names Bieda and Maegla and took no account of the other evidence for Port as an old English personal name, adding that there was at least one other example of the combination of the Saxon word *mutha* with a personal name.[3] His implied contention that a chieftain named Port might after all have landed near a place called Portus is weakened, however, by the appearance immediately afterwards in the Chronicle of entries similarly suggesting that the name of the Isle of Wight (the Roman Vectis) was derived from that of another invading leader, Wihtgar. Perhaps all that can safely or reasonably be said of the entry for 501 is that it may have been based on a vague memory of a landing somewhere in the Ports-mouth region. In that case this landing might have taken place at Portchester, which would have been an ideal place at which to organise resistance such as, it is implied, was offered. Recent excavations there have produced clear evidence of early Saxon occupation in the shape of Saxon pottery of fifth/sixth-century type, but it would be going too far to associate these finds with the legendary landing of Port.

From the fifth to the tenth century there is no documentary evidence relating to Portchester and our knowledge of its history, or rather our deductions about it, must be based solely on the archaeological evidence. This, thanks to further excavations directed by Professor Cunliffe during 1969–71, has now shown that there was some sort of continuous occupation and in the tenth century records began to appear again with increasing frequency. When new pirate-invaders, the Danish Vikings, threatened the coasts of England their tactics of sailing up an inlet or estuary, building a fortified camp on its shore, and commandeering horses on which to ride far and wide on plundering raids must have made Portsmouth Harbour a tempting landing-place. To repel these raids a number of localities, some of which were already surrounded by Roman walls, were fortified or refortified and turned into strongholds (*burhs*) garrisoned by a semi-civilian militia. One of these places was Portchester, which appears as a *burh* in the early tenth century document known as the Burghal Hidage.[4] This implies that its Roman defences were still in a fairly good state of repair, though Professor Cunliffe inclines to the view that the undoubtedly post-Roman Watergate was built about then to repair a breach in the defences which may have been due to the undercutting action of the sea.

At the time of the Domesday Survey in 1086 Portchester was recorded as an ordinary rural manor held by the baron William Maudit and possessing a manorial hall. Since this was probably built before the Norman Conquest it can reasonably be identified with an aisled hall and associated buildings of late Saxon type which have been uncovered by excavation near the centre of the enclosure. How far back before the Conquest these date is uncertain, but it is evident that they continued to be used into the Norman period.

The Norman kings were not slow to realise the possibilities of Portchester. Early in the twelfth century the site passed into royal hands. Henry I was the first to make the harbour his point of departure for Normandy; and when Robert Maudit, who held the office of chamberlain of the treasury, was drowned with Henry's son and heir William in the *White Ship* when returning thence in 1120, leaving only a young daughter, the manor escheated to the crown. True, ten years later another baron, William de Pont de l'Arche, paid a huge sum for the girl's hand and all the lands that went with it; but Henry interpreted the bargain in terms that made William little more than a governor of Portchester on the King's behalf.

By that time Henry had probably begun the work of transforming the old Roman fortress into what in its heyday was one of the three or four great royal castles on the south coast, surpassed only by Dover and Corfe. Documentary evidence for this castle's early history is scanty and there is no specific reference to it before 1153, but its architectural style places it in Henry's reign. By now the timber hall had either fallen into disrepair or been pulled down, but the old Roman walls were still substantially intact and served to enclose the castle's outer bailey. However, since the nine acres they enclosed were too large an area to be made completely secure, an inner bailey was created in their north-west corner, moated on the outside and containing the main buildings of the new fortress, of which the keep or great tower was the earliest and most important. During the next hundred years or so various additions were made, both to strengthen the keep itself and to provide more spacious and comfortable private apartments. These developments served the castle's double function of furnishing a strongpoint for the use of monarchs entering or leaving the country and affording suitable accommodation for royal parties hunting in the neighbouring Forest of Bere. By the later thirteenth century, however, the castle had become hopelessly outdated from a military standpoint. Though repaired in 1296 its fortifications, unlike those of Dover and Corfe, show none of the improvements characteristic of that period. The residential buildings, too, were so ill cared for that a survey in 1274 had described them as antiquated, ruined and unfit for residence.

In Henry I's reign a small Augustinian priory had also been founded within the walls of Portchester in 1133, the church of which still survives, having continued in use when the monks moved away twenty years later to a new priory at Southwick on the other side of Portsdown Hill. Either the occasional close proximity of royalty or—perhaps more probably—the presence of a garrison of rough and no doubt licentious men-at-arms may have been too much for them.

In the fourteenth century the castle was rehabilitated as a royal residence, though it had ceased to be a first-class fortress. The reign of Edward II, who was soon at odds with his barons, saw a new impetus in building at Portchester, thanks largely to his (eventually futile) desire for a retreat where he would be secure from them. There followed at the beginning of the Hundred Years War another hasty and rather superficial refurbishing of the castle in 1338, almost certainly limited to putting the outer defensive circuit into good repair, lest the French should land and sack it as they sacked both Portsmouth and Southampton in that year. Then on the eve of the Crécy campaign in 1346 Edward III stayed in the castle while mustering the force that sailed from the harbour to win that great victory. But as the century wore on the military importance of Portchester declined further, and even though it was still garrisoned against the French it had become obsolete as a military installation by 1400. However since Edward's successor Richard II, like Edward II before him, had fallen out with his barons and therefore wanted a palace that was both secure and up-to-date, it continued to be used as a royal residence though no longer as a fortress. To fit it for this purpose a completely new suite of domestic buildings was erected round the walls of the inner bailey. Contemporary records show not only the great number of workmen employed, but also that at one period some of them had to work by candlelight. But in spite of this sense of urgency Richard was deposed before he could make use of his modernised residence, and the castle soon began to deteriorate again through lack of use and care. Henry V, however, stayed there while preparing the expedition that led to Agincourt, and it was there that what is rather misleadingly called the Southampton Conspiracy was unmasked—the plot to dethrone him in favour of Edmund, Earl of

March, for which the Earl of Cambridge, Lord Scrope of Masham and Sir Thomas Grey paid with their heads.

Thereafter Portchester received little attention for more than a century. From Henry V's time onwards any money for fortification was spent on Portsmouth instead, and by 1441 the castle was reported to be 'ruinous and feeble'. In or about 1527 Henry VIII ordered a naval storehouse to be built within the walls, but at some time before 1585 this was dismantled on the significant ground that it had been superseded by one in Portsmouth, which by now had completely taken over Portchester's naval and military functions. Henry also paid the castle one brief visit; the last English monarch to do so, except for Elizabeth I on one of her progresses in 1601, when she professed herself delighted with everything. In 1632 it ceased to be a royal castle when Charles I sold it to a private owner, Sir William Uvedale, from whom it passed to his relatives the Nortons of Southwick. Subsequently it was brought back into service on at least six occasions by being hired to house prisoners-of-war—Dutchmen in the late seventeenth century and afterwards Frenchmen, mostly seamen, some of whose names can still be seen carved or scratched on the walls. During the Crimean War, which showed up the defects of the British Army's medical services and created a demand for an up-to-date military hospital, the suggestion was put forward that Portchester should be converted to this purpose, but this ill-conceived idea was fortunately quashed.

In 1926 the then owner, Mr A. Thistlethwayte of Southwick Park which is at the foot of the northern slope of Portsdown Hill, transferred the buildings to what is now the Ministry of Public Building and Works. The castle remained part of the Southwick estate, and the local authority was confirmed in the right to use the free space for recreation. Visited yearly by thousands of people for this purpose or because of its historical interest, the ruins of the old Roman fortress, enclosing the medieval church and castle, still stand four-square, looking across the water to the city and the naval base which have long supplanted them.

2. Portsmouth in the Middle Ages

The Norman Conquest, besides reviving the importance of Portchester, brought Portsmouth itself into existence, though not immediately. In the Domesday Survey its name does not figure at all, and only three settlements on the island on which it was to arise and which was later to be called Portsea are mentioned—Buckland, Copnor and Frodding-ton (the modern Fratton).[1] The soil of the island was mostly un-productive, being sand or gravel in the southern part and clay in the northern, and its total population can have amounted only to two or three hundred peasants. But now that the other side of the Channel ceased for a century and a half to be a hostile shore, Norman and Plantagenet monarchs whose true homelands lay in France and who were therefore frequently travelling from one part of their dominions to another were constantly landing in or leaving from the harbour. It was on one such occasion that Henry I, while waiting for a wind, had been so struck by its advantages that he had decided to build a castle within the walls of Portchester. These royal visits led presently, perhaps through the growing difficulty of reaching those walls by water when the northern part of the harbour began to silt up, to the growth of a settlement at the mouth of the port, in the south-western corner of the island.[2]

By the 1180s, although this settlement was still very small, it was nevertheless large enough to need a church. On the manor of Buckland (by then called Portsea) one had already arisen by 1166 where the modern St Mary's at Kingston stands;* but the first church of Ports-mouth proper was begun about fifteen years later when John of Gisors, a wealthy merchant and shipowner, granted an acre of land to the monks of the Augustinian priory which had come into existence at Southwick, whereon to build a chapel dedicated to the recently martyred Archbishop Thomas à Becket.[3] This church continued to be administered by Southwick Priory till the Reformation brought about

---

* There is documentary evidence for the existence of a vicar of Portsea in 1166, and the grant of a church there by Baldwin de Portsea to Southwick Priory in 1170 evidently relates to the refounding of an earlier place of worship (R. HUBBOCK, *Portsea Island Churches*, p. 3).

the dissolution of the religious houses in the sixteenth century, after which the trust was transferred to Winchester College. Parts of the church, though greatly altered and enlarged, survive to-day in what is now the cathedral of St Thomas, which thus may claim to be in a way the oldest building on the island.[4]

Yet the true founder of Portsmouth as a town, however tiny, was Richard the Lion-Heart. At the beginning of his reign he had set out on a crusade, during which he had quarrelled with King Philip Augustus of France and on his way back from which he had been captured by Duke Leopold of Austria and held to ransom. As soon as he returned to England in 1194 he summoned a fleet and army to Portsmouth Harbour, vowing vengeance on Philip and his other enemies. But for this he needed money, and among his methods of raising it was the grant or rather sale of charters of privileges to various places. Among them was the settlement that we may henceforth call Portsmouth, which he had taken over from John of Gisors and where his fleet was now delayed by unfavourable winds. While the King chafed and sought to pass the time by hunting in the nearby Forest of Stansted the inhabitants seized a favourable moment to secure a charter entitling them to an annual fair lasting fifteen days, a market every Thursday, the right to settle petty suits and try minor offences in courts of their own instead of having to go to those of the hundred or shire, and to pay a 'farm' of £18 a year—exemption, that is, from the numerous ill-defined and expandable exactions of the royal officials in return for paying this annual lump sum as the 'farm of the borough' which they could collect themselves. At the fair, which came to be known as the Free Mart Fair, all comers, whether natives or foreigners, were (as was usual at such fairs) to be exempt from all dues, tolls or other impositions, as well as from arrest for debt. A large device of an open hand, symbolising the welcome and good fellowship that strangers might expect, was displayed in the High Street, where the fair was held, during its continuance. Since the King's seal with which the charter was sealed had a crescent and an eight-pointed star (as had the seal of his chancellor, Bishop William de Longchamps of Ely, by whose hand the charter was 'given') it is widely believed that the presence of these emblems in the city's coat of arms is due to this circumstance. There is, however, no documentary evidence to support this belief, and the star and crescent was a device much in use about this time.[5]

Besides letting out land to individuals to build on, Richard himself had houses built at Portsmouth, on the improvement of which and of his *curia* or hall there £2 18s 3d was spent in 1197–8. The site of this latter building is thought to have been marked later by the name of Kingshall Green in Penny Street, where in more modern times the Clarence Barracks were erected.[6]

In 1200, soon after his accession, Richard's brother and successor John confirmed the charter of 1194. He too used Portsmouth a great deal, making it the point of departure of his expeditions and landing there when he returned to England. When he allowed the bulk of his French provinces to slip from his hands a new phase of its history may be said to have begun. To regain these provinces became an object of English policy, and John could hardly avoid becoming something of a precursor of the Royal Navy. There were few 'king's ships' as yet, and the Cinque Ports of Dover, Hastings, Romney, Hythe and Sandwich* had hitherto been called on when a fighting fleet was needed. But these ports, always rather small for the concentration of a large force, were beginning to silt up, and Portsmouth (and Southampton) were in any case better placed for a descent on Normandy. It was therefore now that Portsmouth first—though very tentatively—began to be a naval base. It was already the practice to beach ships there for repair in a creek called the Pond of the Abbess (since the windmill on its southern shore belonged to the Abbess of Fontevrault). This creek ran inland from the harbour, close to where the *Vernon* torpedo establishment is today, to near the present Guildhall Square, and had been dammed up to provide the head-water for a mill, on account of which it came to be known later as the Mill Pond. It was also called the Great Lake, and ultimately gave its name to Lake Road, up which tradition says that its waters flowed until comparatively modern times. It was here that most of the shipping of the port anchored after discharging cargo at the little nearby haven called the Camber which also ran in from the harbour, or before setting out on a voyage.[7] As a trading port Portsmouth was a mere member or adjunct of Southampton, and it was therefore to the sheriff of that town that John addressed a command in 1212 to enclose the 'docks' or mudflats on which this beaching and those repairs took place with a 'good and strong wall' and also to build penthouses and store-houses in which the ships' tackle might be safely kept. The actual work of constructing what is generally considered Portsmouth's first dock was carried out by the Archdeacon of Taunton, William of Wrotham, who held the office of Keeper of the King's Ships in that age when such secular and even quasi-military appointments were often filled by clerics because of their near-monopoly of the ability to read and write.[8]

It was probably also about 1212 that another and greater ecclesiastic, Pierre des Roches, a very able Poitevin whom John had made Bishop of Winchester and was shortly to make his justiciar or chief justice, founded the *Domus Dei* or Hospital of St Nicholas, which was completed early in the next reign as an almshouse and a hospice for travellers. It was staffed by a Master, who was sometimes a layman, six monks and six nuns, who were charged to look after the poor and sick and to receive pilgrims and other travellers through the port who might be in need of lodging. These duties it performed for over 300

---

* To which Winchelsea and Rye came to be added.

years until it shared the fate of other religious houses at Henry VIII's hands and was surrendered to his commissioners in 1540. For twenty years after that some of the building was used as an armoury; then with Portsmouth's development as a fortress it became the residence of the military governor, though the chapel remained in religious use and it was here that Charles II married the Portuguese princess Catherine of Braganza in 1662. Afterwards the buildings fell into disrepair until little but the chapel survived, but this was restored in 1867–8 to become the Garrison Church.[9]

It was also early in the reign of John's successor Henry III that Portsmouth's first dock ended its short life. Its site had not been well chosen, since in spite of the sheltered character of most of these waters it was relatively exposed to wind and tide; and in 1228 an order was given to block it up.[10] Nevertheless the port continued to be a mustering-place of fleets and armies. From it Henry III sailed on several of his unsuccessful expeditions against France, and it was here that the future Edward I embarked when—rather unwisely in the heir to a somewhat troubled crown—he went on a crusade in 1270. After his accession, too, he used it as a base against Gascony; and when he tried to conquer Scotland he assembled a fleet here to guard against an attack by the French in his rear.[11]

The consequent coming and going, from time to time, of ships from most of the maritime towns of England, transporting men and horses, provisions and arms, brought trade into the town; in addition to which it carried on some traffic with the western and northern countries of Europe. Despite the rivalry of Southampton the export of wool and grain increased. Wheat was exported to France and Spain, and the wool trade was at least large enough for Portsmouth to be among the fifty-seven towns summoned to send wool merchants to consult with the King at York in 1327–8. The chief import was wine, mostly from Bayonne and Bordeaux; while a good deal of woad was also imported from Normandy, and wax and iron from France. Nevertheless the vessels belonging to the port were evidently few and small as yet, for when it was summoned at the beginning of the Hundred Years War to send to the King's aid all ships which were capable of carrying over forty *dolia* of wine it could produce only two, and one of these was out of repair.[12]

The fact that the little port was legally only a part of that of Southampton, whose eastern limits stretched beyond it to Langstone Harbour, had meant that before the gift of Richard I's charter the men of that town had collected the customary dues or 'customs' from any ships that loaded or unloaded in Portsmouth Harbour. After 1194 they collected only the greater or national customs, on wool, wool-fells and leather, while the petty customs or minor local imposts were taken and retained by Portsmouth's own officials, £7 being deducted from the farm of the borough of Southampton in consideration of this. It might be more accurate, however, to say that this was the general outline of a situation whose details and implications were much disputed between the two towns until in 1239 an agreement was made between them by which only the harbour of Portsmouth was to be Southampton's sphere and the local customs were to be shared equally between them. Even this, however, by no means put an end to disputation. Towards the close of the sixteenth century Portsmouth made a determined effort to shake off altogether its dependence on Southampton in the matter of customs by proposing to erect a customs house in its own port. This greatly alarmed the Sotonians, who feared that Sussex and a great part of Hampshire, hitherto usually served with wines, woad, canvas and other commodities from their own town, would henceforward be provided with them by Portsmouth. But in spite of the compilation in 1572 of a list of arguments or 'allegations why Portsmouth should have no customs house', a draft of which survives in the Southampton records, the rival town apparently made good its bid for independence in practice. The matter was not finally laid to rest, however, until the Municipal Reform Act of 1835 formally abolished Southampton's jurisdiction within the port of Portsmouth.[13]

The earliest known government of medieval Portsmouth seems to have been by a reeve and bailiffs. William of Sainte-Mère Eglise, who accounted for the petty customs when they were first separated from those of Southampton, may have been the first reeve. The number of bailiffs is so far unknown; but probably, as at Winchester, there were two. In John's reign it was they who collected the rents and petty customs and were responsible to the crown for the farm of the borough. Cases were tried before them, and their duties also included the sealing of conveyances of land with the town seal, the earliest known form of which is said to date from the thirteenth century and shows a single-masted vessel on the waves, with mainsail furled and the crescent and star above it. In due course the reeve faded out and the bailiffs acted for the town; a royal writ was addressed to them in 1224, and subsequent writs were sent to 'the bailiffs and men of Portsmouth' or simply to 'the men of Portsmouth'. Later again the mayor appeared. The 'customs and usages' of the town, drawn up in a custumal assigned to the later thirteenth century, were compiled by a mayor (if the rather uncertain translation of a lost original document may be accepted on this point), one bailiff, constables, serjeants (or subordinate officers) and jurats (which may be rendered sworn councillors). The first unmistakeable reference to the office of mayor, however, dates from 1323, when a writ was addressed to the mayor and bailiffs of Portsmouth. The bailiffs continued in existence long after the introduction of the mayoral office, and in Elizabeth I's charter of incorporation* it was

---

* See below, p. 35.

stated that the town had formerly been governed by a mayor, two bailiffs, two constables and other public officers.[14]

At first no definite allowance was made to the mayor from the town funds, but he had certain perquisites such as the right to receive two bushels of wheat from every boatload brought into port and to take for himself certain fines levied in the town courts. In 1543 these last were commuted for an annual payment to be settled at his election, which presently became a regular £30, reduced to £20 in the late seventeenth century. Then in 1671 this was exchanged for the use of the butchers' shambles and the loft above them; and in 1785 it was arranged that all the mayor's former perquisites should be thrown into the common fund, from which his expenses up to £300 a year were to be paid.[15]

In 1256 the town was granted a guild merchant; the right, that is, to form an association of its more substantial traders for mutual aid and profit. The privileges membership conferred were mainly commercial and included the exclusive right of buying goods within the town in order to sell them again in it (in other words a profitable monopoly of the position of middlemen in many transactions), together with the sole rights of buying certain commodities within the town for any purpose at all or at any time except on market or fair days. Guildsmen likewise had the first opportunity to bargain for any merchandise brought to the town for sale and the right of claiming a share in any good bargain made by a fellow-member; in addition to which they were exempt from petty customs. Membership of the guild could be inherited by a guildsman's eldest son, bought (which was normally the only avenue open to his younger brothers) or occasionally granted to outsiders or even foreigners who had lived in the town for a number of years and contributed to its finances by paying scot and lot, which may be very roughly translated as rates and taxes. In effect the guild authorities governed the trade of the town while the civic officers governed it in other respects; but since they were very liable to be the same persons a merger inevitably took place, here as elsewhere, in the course of time. The details of this gradual process have usually remained obscure, and in Portsmouth's case they are particularly so owing to the loss of the earlier town records; but it was certainly 'the mayor and burgesses' (the latter originally a rather indeterminate term which in the early thirteenth century signified leading citizens but afterwards came to mean guildsmen) who regulated the trade in the sixteenth and following centuries, and it was in the Guildhall that they held the town courts.[16]

The oldest of these courts were probably the court leet and view of frankpledge. Their business included the supervision of weights and measures and the trial of such offences as encroachments, fights and bloodshed, and commercial offences such as using false weights or charging more than the maximum prices laid down for certain commodities. The court leet seems also to have dealt with such matters as the admission of tenants to the town lands. In later times its criminal work was largely taken over by the justices of the peace. A court of piepowder was also held during fair time to settle disputes arising at the Fair and try offences committed there, but it fell out of use as the Fair deteriorated towards the end of the eighteenth century.[17]

The jurisdiction of the borough, according to the late thirteenth-century custumal mentioned above, extended or rather was claimed to extend over the whole harbour.[18] One result of this was a Chancery suit brought in 1435 by John Mathew, deputy to the Lord Admiral, against the bailiff and burgesses of Portsmouth for assaulting him and preventing him from holding a court of admiralty in the borough. Although the versions of what happened naturally differ, it seems that when he attempted to do so the bailiff showed him a copy of the town charter to support the claim that the town was outside admiralty jurisdiction and when he declined to accept this contention, he was asked to delay while an appeal was made to the Lord Chancellor on the point. The deputy agreed to this, but nevertheless held a court at the waterside some time later, which was interrupted by the arrival of the bailiff with a serjeant and some constables. A struggle followed, and when it was wrongly reported that the bailiff had been killed the whole town came rushing to the spot and the deputy had to be escorted to his lodging by the bailiff's officers. In the fracas, he complained, not only had the King's books been cast to the ground, but he had 'never yet found a purse of black leather, in which was £13 in gold [a large sum then] ... and a seal of office'. The issue in dispute remained unsettled and arose again from time to time.[19] On land, according to a perambulation of the borough and its liberties in 1566, it seems that its jurisdiction extended as far north as a line from Tipner to the Green Post on the London road, and as far east as the bounds of Copnor, Kingston and Fratton, while the sea formed the southern boundary.[20]

To the Model Parliament of 1295 Portsmouth returned two burgesses, and from then to the present day it has sent members to all but a few parliaments. Most of these exceptions occurred in the fourteenth century, probably because of the burden caused by their expenses, which fell either on the chosen representatives or on all the burgesses. Until at least the close of the Middle Ages, as far as can be deduced from the surviving returns, only the bailiffs and burgesses had a voice in Parliamentary elections, and it has been calculated—admittedly no more recently than 1835—that in the fifteenth and sixteenth centuries there were never more than thirteen of the latter.[21]

Before this, as late as the fourteenth century, the town was no bigger than a fair-sized modern village, with a few side-lanes opening out of the High Street and scattered homesteads in large plots of ground extending on all sides. Nearly all the houses were of wood; only the church and the *Domus Dei* escaped the fire when the French burned the town in 1338.[22] To the north and east stretched the common fields, for despite the growing trade agriculture was still the people's main occupation. 'In times of distress', the Hundred Rolls recorded, 'the town is sometimes comparatively deserted'.[23]

Such times of distress were mainly due to the attacks of enemies, both English and foreign. First of all it was sacked and burnt by the men of the Cinque Ports in 1265, during the Barons' Wars which arose from Simon de Montfort's opposition to Henry III.[24] But it was the repeated devastations by the French in the fourteenth century which caused by far the most damage. The town was still unwalled and quite unfortified, and the inhabitants were almost ruined by the assaults they suffered after the outbreak of the Hundred Years War in 1338. Again and again the place was sacked and the wooden houses clustering round the church and the *Domus Dei* were burnt by the foe. In 1338 itself a French fleet under Nicholas Béhuchet came over flying English flags and landed men before anyone realised that they were hostile. The inhabitants of both sexes and all ages were slaughtered together with their livestock, and their dwellings were razed to the ground. A similar surprise was achieved at Southampton, but whereas that town, hitherto almost equally unfortified, afterwards surrounded itself with walls of solid stone, Portsmouth was too shattered to do this. In vain Edward III allowed the town exemption from military taxation in the immediate future 'for the poverty which they are undergoing in these days',[25] while commanding its authorities to levy a tax on merchandise entering the port for the next eight years in order to raise money for building stone walls. Although a little trade in wool and wine somehow struggled into life again, it was too slight and the population too diminished for the money to be got together, especially since the customs dues were still being collected in part by officers from Southampton, so that traders often found themselves liable to double taxation and hence fought shy of Portsmouth altogether. Only enough was collected to build some very insufficient mud and timber ramparts which gave little security, and with these the town had to rest content.[26]

Although it was from Portsmouth that the great expedition which led to the splendid victory of Crècy sailed in 1346, the port was able to contribute to it only a very few ships and men.[27] Two years later the plague known as the Black Death struck, wiping out not only whole families but almost whole trades; and then in 1369, 1377 and 1380 the town was sacked again, in the last case without any resistance being offered. This, however, was the nadir of ignominy; when in 1383 the French fitted out five balingers* to prevent communication between England and the English army which was then in Flanders, it was the men of Portsmouth and Dartmouth who armed their ships and after a stiff fight captured all five; and when two years later a French fleet collected at Sluys and threatened invasion the only blow struck in reply came again from the men of these two ports, who sailed to the Seine with

---

* A balinger was a kind of sloop

a small force and attacked such ships as they found there, sinking four and taking four more.[28]

At the turn of the century, though there was no formal war between England and France, piracy was rife on both sides of the Channel and crews of desperadoes issued from Portsmouth as well as from Dover, Rye, Poole, Plymouth and other towns to prey on former foes and neutrals alike. Prominent among the worst offenders was the Portsmuthian Henry Spicer, who with several others was summoned before the King's Council in 1403, but apparently without result.[29]

Even so, in view of Portsmouth's sufferings it is hardly surprising that in the later part of the fourteenth century the fleets of England were more often asssembled at stone-girt Southampton. In the early fifteenth century, indeed, it became for a brief space the country's principal naval port and might conceivably have remained so, while Portsmouth sank into a purely mercantile community; though when Mr David Lloyd speculates that although it had some trade and had been the scene of some military movements it 'could well have relapsed into the obscurity of a New Romney, a Hythe or a Winchelsea with nothing but a fine church to tell of a period of prosperity'[30] he perhaps hardly allows enough for the superiority of its natural advantages over theirs. In the fifteenth century, however, its potentialities as a naval base began to be realised. It is true that when the Hundred Years War flared up again in Henry V's reign and the King determined to enlarge his navy and develop a base that should challenge and outdo some recent French developments at Rouen he chose Southampton and the River Hamble because they had suffered less of late, and that the most important of the ships he added to his navy were built there.[31] Nevertheless he did not entirely neglect Portsmouth, for it was in 1418, during his reign, that a wooden Round Tower began to be built at the mouth of the harbour to strengthen the defences. This, the first of the port's permanent defensive works, was completed about 1426. Opposite it on the Gosport side of the harbour a similar tower was built at the same time or perhaps a little later.[32]

After Henry's early death his plans for Southampton were abandoned and for most of the long and feeble reign of his son Henry VI there practically ceased to be a royal navy at all. When in 1442 eight large and sixteen smaller ships were levied for the national defence the total contribution of Hampshire consisted of one balinger with a crew of forty.[33] A last revival in 1449 of the war with France, which was flickering out in failure, involved once more the gathering of ships and men at Portsmouth. But the discontented and mutinous attitude of the sailors, who resented bitterly the neglect of their pay and provisions, caused delay and one of the most unpopular of the King's advisers, Bishop Adam Moleyns of Chichester, was sent to Portsmouth in 1450 to pay and appease them. When the seamen, who already held him responsible for defeats abroad and slowness in sending reinforcements, found that he had brought only part of their long-overdue wages, they burst into the *Domus Dei* where he was conducting a service, dragged him out and murdered him. For this heinous crime against the church the Pope placed the town under the Greater Excommunication (sometimes loosely referred to as an interdict), which prohibited the celebration of mass and all other liturgical ceremonies, the ringing of church bells, the public administration of the sacraments and burial in consecrated ground. Whether or not these dread penalties were really enforced in full for more than half a century, it was only in 1508 that the excommunication was lifted through the intercession of the powerful Bishop Fox of Winchester; and then only after an elaborate ceremony of penance in which the vicar of St Thomas's and many of his parishioners were first scourged barefoot out of the church with rods and only readmitted after they had prostrated themselves before the Bishop's representatives and suffered further chastisement at their hands. The town was then pardoned, the church cleansed with purifying vapour, and high mass sung. As part of the penance a chantry chapel was ordered to be built on a spot between the *Domus Dei* and the Square Tower which had been erected a few years earlier at the seaward end of the High Street. After the dissolution of the chantries in 1547, however, it was converted into a storehouse.[34]

3. Tudor Portsmouth: progress and a setback

The accession of the Tudors in 1485 proved all-important for Portsmouth. Under Henry VII, the first Tudor monarch, large sums were spent on its defences. The Round Tower was rebuilt in stone, and a little further towards the sea on the eastern shore of the harbour mouth a Square Tower at the seaward end of the High Street and just beyond it a Great (or as it was later called, a Saluting) Platform were built—or completed, since both may have been begun earlier. Although the Square Tower was designed primarily as a military fortification it came presently to serve as the residence of the Governor, as the commander of the garrison which was established in the next reign was called, and after 1580 it was converted into a powder magazine and used as such till the middle of the eighteenth century. The Platform was rebuilt in 1568, but in spite of this it was in such bad shape again by 1585 that it was thought inadvisable to fire a salute from it on the anniversary of Elizabeth I's coronation lest it should tumble down altogether.[1]

Henry's great service to Portsmouth, however, was to institute the dockyard by ordering a dry or graving dock to be built into which vessels could be floated to have their bottoms cleaned by scraping or burning and then coated with tar. Hitherto ships which needed cleaning or repairs had been floated as high up as possible on to mud-flats, after which the tide was allowed to leave them and temporary walls or fences were built round them. Latterly the River Hamble, which falls into Southampton Water near its mouth, had been much used for this purpose; but Henry's two latest and heaviest ships, the *Regent* and the *Sovereign*, drew too much water to be drawn up there in this way. In 1495–6, therefore, Robert Brygandine the Clerk of the King's Ships, with the advice of Sir Reginald Bray the King's chief architect and the builder of Windsor Castle, constructed the dock about half a mile up-harbour from the town, where high and low water marks came close together and a peninsula of dry land projected into the deep water of the harbour. At no other undeveloped site on its shore could the dual advantages of

eep water and firm ground for buildings have been found to-
ether. The dock was made of timber, with inner and outer gates, and
hen a ship had entered it the water was pumped or drawn out of it by
horse-driven 'engine' and bucket contrivance, after which the space
etween the gates was apparently filled up with stones and clay. A
torehouse, forge and smithy were added, at a total cost of £193 0 6¾.[2]
This was the final parting of the ways between Portsmouth and South-
mpton, for henceforth the former became primarily a naval port and
he latter exclusively mercantile.

Not that Henry VII ever intended to build a great war navy; he had
o need of one and it was not in his character to spend money on
nything unnecessary. What he wanted was to encourage shipbuilding
nd trade, and to that end he built royal ships which, before the distinc-
ion between warships and armed merchantmen developed in the next
eign, could be used for commerce in time of peace and in case of war
ould form a nucleus round which private ships could rally to make up a
ghting fleet. Two such, the *Sweepstake* and the *Mary Fortune*, were
uilt at Portsmouth later, though they were comparatively small
essels.[3]

Under Henry VIII the King's ships developed both in number and
ize, and the specialised fighting ship came into existence, giving Henry
is title to be considered the founder of the Royal Navy. Genuinely and
leeply interested in naval matters, he was determined to keep abreast of
r outrival France, which had lately fortified Le Havre. In the first of
is three wars with France, Portsmouth was used as the rendezvous
or the English fleet and the base for a cross-Channel attack.[4] The
lockyard was kept busy and it was from it that the finest of the King's
ew ships was launched, the *Mary Rose* named after his younger sister.
The defences of the town were gradually improved, the mud walls
eing strengthened and guns mounted on them; a military garrison was
nstituted, four brewhouses were built to supply beer for an expedition
gainst Gascony; and at the beginning of the second war, in 1522–3, a
reat chain of iron was made which could be stretched across the mouth
f the harbour from the Round Tower to its counterpart on the Gosport
ide. During that war, too, the dockyard was enlarged to accommodate a
till larger and finer ship than the *Mary Rose*, the *Henri Grace à Dieu*. In
527 came a further extension, when nine acres of land were bought, and
nany buildings grew up round the dock. Then when some of the money
lerived from the dissolution of the monasteries was being spent on
uilding forts along the south and east coasts as defences against
nvasion, came the construction of a fort afterwards called Southsea
Castle,* on the shore about a mile to the east of the Round Tower.[5]

---

* In contemporary records it was variously called Portsea Castle,
the castle at Portsmouth and the Southsea Castle (MRS W. J. GUY,
Historic Portsmouth, p. 5).

But while Portsmouth had certain advantages as a base for cross
Channel enterprises—a rendezvous for fleets and armies, a shipbuilding
and repairing centre, a harbour of refuge and a lying-up resort for ships
in winter—it had serious disadvantages also, in its distance from
London and its lack of shipwrights and other skilled labour. Its slow
growth and comparatively small merchant class, moreover, made it
unable to supply victuals for a fleet, and when one had to be provisioned
there the supplies had to come from Southampton. As for shipbuilding
labour, in the early sixteenth century there was no large supply of this in
any district, but it was scattered over a considerable number of small
private yards on the south, east and west coasts. When Brygandine was
building the first dry dock he had to ride into Kent to the Cinque Ports
to get the carpenters and smiths he needed; and in order to bring
together the hundreds of men required to build one of Henry VIII's
ships or to fit out one of his fleets recourse was had to impressment
which continued to be used for this purpose long after the dockyard
establishments had been put on a permanent footing.* Yards could not
however, be run efficiently by employing comparatively large numbers
of men for short periods and then discharging them; ships might be
built or fleets prepared for sea by such methods, but regular programmes
of repair and refitting would have been impossible. Henry VIII or his
advisers seem to have been alive to this and to the consequent need to
employ a permanent nucleus staff, since from 1538 onwards he gave
annuities to men who carried out the duties of master shipwrights, if
they did not bear the name. Nevertheless even at the end of Elizabeth's
reign the total permanent nucleus staff of the royal yards was still small
and at Portsmouth it was microscopic.[6]

But it was mainly Portsmouth's shortcomings as a source of supply of
the materials ships needed, in contrast with London, that brought other
dockyards into existence on the Thames and Medway which presently
eclipsed their predecessor for a long period. The cost of carrying stores
to Portsmouth was held to be prohibitive, whereas London could
provide pitch, tar and oakum more cheaply; iron from the Kentish
Weald was available without the long haul across Hampshire to bring it
from the Weald of Sussex to Portsmouth; and timber could very easily
be carried down the Thames. Moreover for various reasons the Medway
then seemed more convenient as an anchorage. Before the middle of
Henry VIII's reign, therefore, yards were rising at Woolwich and
Deptford to dispute Portsmouth's supremacy, and it was at Woolwich
that the *Henri Grace à Dieu* was built.

About 1540 John Leland, who travelled extensively throughout the
country between 1535 and 1545, came to Portsmouth, of which he left a

---

* Warrants for pressing shipwrights for work at Portsmouth and
other yards were issued as late as 1708.

description wherein, besides the towers on either side of the harbour mouth, the 'mighty chain of iron' that could be drawn between them, the dock and the walls, he noted the 'gate of timber at the north-east end of the town' (at the top of the High Street) which was the principal entrance and the bastion recently built to protect this—'an hill of earth ditched, wherein be guns to defend entry into the town by land'.[7] This outwork was known as the Town Mount, and was protected by a moat. About fifty years later the gate, which had come to be called the Landport, was moved westward to a position which a successor built in 1760 still occupies, though after the disappearance of the fortifications it now serves as an entrance to the United Services Recreation Ground. It was at the Landport Gate that the ceremony of presenting the keys of the fortress of Portsmouth to visiting English sovereigns took place. They were handed by the Governor to the monarch and immediately returned with the command to 'open the gates of His [or Her] Majesty's fortress'.[8] This ceremony was last enacted, not here but on the Guildhall steps, when Elizabeth II came to open the rebuilt Guildhall in 1959. When the Portsmouth garrison was closed in the following year a controversy arose because the keys were claimed by Gosport on the ground that the nearest Army quarters were now there; but by Her Majesty's permission they are deposited in the Guildhall in the city's care.

Leland went on to add that there was much vacant ground within the town wall (as illustration no. 4 shows), 'one fair street from west to north-east' (the High Street) and but one parish church. In the middle of the High Street, he continued, 'one Carpenter, a rich man, made of late time . . . a town house'. The builder of this first Town Hall was mayor in 1531 and 1537, but nothing is known of the form of the building save that it is supposed to have been a timber structure.[9]

At this time three or four miles of open country lay between Portsbridge, which crossed the creek that separated Portsea Island from the mainland, and the little village of Kingston. Here the road divided, the left-hand fork leading past St Mary's Church to Buckland and Froddington, with the hamlets of Copnor and Middleton (Milton) lying to the east, while the other or main road passed over Kingston Heath and then between the town fields of Portsmouth on the left and the dock fields on the right, to the Landport Gate. To the west of the dock fields lay Portsmouth Common, which with the Mill Pond separated the town from the dockyard.[10]

In 1544 Henry VIII's third war with France broke out, and in retaliation for the English capture of Boulogne (which they held only for eight years) the French in the following year gathered a great armada for a counterstroke and made a landing at Brading in the Isle of Wight, while their fleet under D'Annebault the Lord Admiral of France lay off St Helen's, threatening the English fleet at Spithead under Lord Lisle. Henry himself was aboard his fleet, having come down to

Portsmouth with the double purpose of inspecting his new fort at Southsea and reviewing the army encamped on Southsea Common, which had been collected to repel the French. He was in fact feasting with Lisle and his officers in the flagship which bore his name when the alarm was given that D'Annebault's ships were rounding St Helen's Point. Henry was hastily put ashore and stood, 'fretting and his teeth on edge', for there was little wind and whereas he had pinned his faith to sailing ships the van of the French consisted of about thirty oared galleys which were independent of the wind and each armed with a large gun in the bows. The English had been taken by surprise and at a disadvantage. For a time the galleys bombarded them almost without reply, though at long range, but presently the wind began to serve and they got under way, though not without a great disaster. The *Mary Rose*, whose open gunports were only about 16 or 18 inches above the water-level, filled and sank, either because of a slight list or according to one account because she had heeled over while tacking after firing a broadside in order to fire another. Whichever was correct, it is probable that a contributory or even prime cause was the clumsiness and indiscipline of her crew; her Captain Sir George Carew had called out just before the catastrophe to his brother in another ship that he had 'too many knowledgeable mariners on board, who each thought they knew best'. Carew and nearly all the ship's company of over five hundred, including Sir Richard Grenville's grandfather, perished. But since the French hesitated to close with the English, perhaps from fear of a number of row-barges which had now come out from Portsmouth Harbour and inflicted considerable damage on the galleys, while the English on their part were reluctant to advance beyond the shelter of their fortifications, the action was tactically indecisive. Strategically it served the English purpose, for the French would not venture a landing in force on the mainland and after a few days' plundering of the Isle of Wight they sailed away.[11]

When Henry VIII died in 1547 the relative importance of Portsmouth as a naval station was diminishing. Ships were sent round from there to lie in the Medway, and for some years the expenditure at the dockyard was very small; between 1547 and 1551 it was not only well below that at Deptford and Woolwich but even below that at Gillingham as well.[12] The defences, though they had impressed Leland, failed on the whole to pass the more critical and professional inspection of two commissioners sent down by Henry's young son and successor Edward VI, who reported that the Round Tower had no guns and no men to man them if there had been any, that its counterpart at Blockhouse on the Gosport side was still merely wooden, that the guns on Portsmouth's walls were few and inadequate, that the defences came to an end well before St Thomas's Street, leaving the northern arm of the Camber quite undefended, and finally that though the dockyard was encircled by a mud and timber wall this had no guns on it.[13]

1 Air view of Portchester Castle *Photo: A. W. Rule*

2 Plan of Portchester Castle

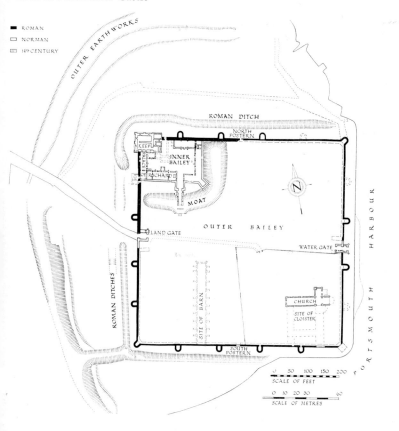

3 Portsmouth in 1545 from an engraving by James Basire published in 1778 and made from a contemporary wall painting formerly in Cowdray House, near Midhurst. *Portsmouth City Museums*

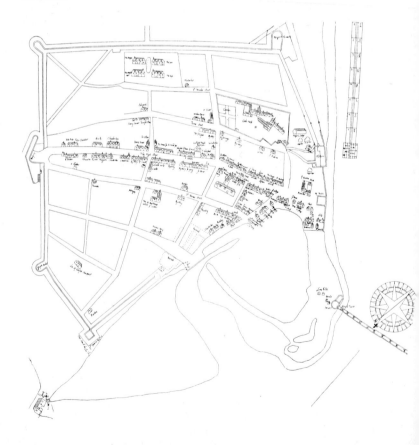

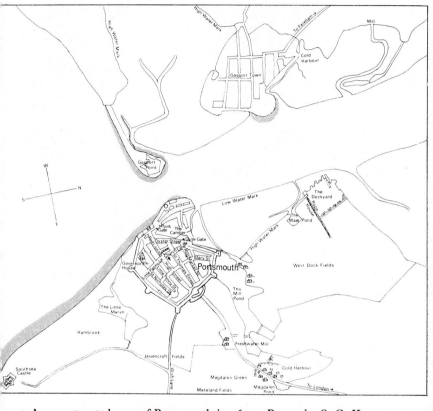

5 A reconstructed map of Portsmouth in 1659 *Drawn by S. G. Kerry*

Ancient plan of the town of Portsmouth made in the reign of Elizabeth I

George Villiers, Duke of Buckingham, painting by Daniel Mytens.
Reproduced by gracious permission of Her Majesty The Queen

King James' Gate built in 1687 as viewed from Point. The archway
on the right of the picture was added in the nineteenth century.
Portsmouth City Museums

The Landport Gate, c. 1717   *Portsmouth City Museums*

1. Landport Gate
2. Landport Curtine
3. Landport Barracks
4. Landport Guard
5. Bridge over the Main Moat
6. The Ravelin
7. Guard-house to the Ravelin
8. Bridge to the Ravelin

A PROSPECT of the *LANDPORT GATE*
and *BRIDGE* with the *RAVELIN*
before it, at
~PORTSMOUTH~
as it appears from the *CAVALIER* on *TOWN BASTION*

9. Main Moat
10. Guys Bastion
11. Grand Storehouse
12. Dock Chappel
13. The Common
14. Ports Down
15. Inward Coverd way
16. Glacis

9 A South-East view of Portsmouth; engraving
by Waters, 1765   *Portsmouth City Museums*

10 John Carter, 1715–1794, from a painting; artist
and date unknown   *Portsmouth City Museums*

11 Royal Naval Academy, Portsmouth   *Portsmouth City Museums*

12. Portsmouth Point, an etching by Thomas Rowlandson
National Maritime Museum, London

13 Earl Howe ('Black Dick'), from a painting by John Singleton Copley
National Maritime Museum, London

This report prompted the young and delicate but precocious king to visit the town himself. To a friend, Barnaby Fitzpatric, he wrote

We . . . viewed not only the town itself and the haven, but also divers bulwarks. In viewing of which we find the bulwarks chargeable [i.e., expensive], massy, well rampared, but ill fashioned, ill flanked and set in unmeet places, the town weak in comparison of what it ought to be, though great (for within the walls are fair and large closes and much vacant room),* the haven notable great and standing by nature easy to be fortified.[14]

Nothing, however, was done to improve the defences before Edward's premature death a year later in 1553. Nor were things much better at first under his half-sister Mary, who never visited Portsmouth during her equally short reign. Towards its close, however, war broke out again with France and led to increased activity in all the dockyards.At Portsmouth, where a fire in 1557 had destroyed the storehouses, wharves and new storehouses were built, stores provided and ships stationed.[15]

After Elizabeth's accession the work of strengthening the fortifications was pushed forward and continued intermittently throughout her long reign. The Earls of Arundel and Sussex, who were in charge of the royal forests in the area, were instructed to supply the timber needed for the extension and repair of the ramparts,[16] and in 1569 the first public lottery in England (though they were well enough known in the Netherlands) was instituted to provide funds for this and similar work at other ports. There were 400,000 lots, each costing ten shillings, a large sum for those days, which proved a fatal error of judgement, for although the prizes were good the tickets did not sell well enough and the scheme failed.[17] Nevertheless the ramparts and the moat around the town were completely reshaped according to the latest principles of military engineering under the guidance of Richard Popinjay, who was Surveyor of Portsmouth from 1560 to 1589. The work went slowly at first, but when relations with Spain worsened and the threat of invasion loomed a peak of activity was reached. The semi-circular bastions of the earlier part of the century were rebuilt in an arrowhead form which by protecting guns that were mounted on a level with the moat facilitated a flanking fire and so gave greater coverage of the curtain walls.[18] A new defence for the Camber was provided by a strong stone wall across the neck of Point, the little peninsula projecting between it and the harbour mouth which had long been recognised as potentially vulnerable to a close attack. A picket fence with a fortified gateway had previously been erected across this neck, probably in the fifteenth century, and then replaced in Henry VIII's later years by a wall of gabions (large round

---

* Cf. Leland. This was true of most towns then and for long afterwards.

wicker baskets filled with earth), for which this stone wall was substituted.[19] All hedges, buildings and other obstacles to a clear field of
fire within fifty yards of the ramparts were removed, and ditches
deepened. It was the maintenance of this insistence on an unobstructed
field of fire for centuries which gave Portsmouth its peculiar urban
pattern; both it and later its satellite Portsea grew up within these
constricting fortifications, with a belt of unbuilt-on land around each of
them, while their eighteenth- and nineteenth-century suburbs developed
apart from the parent towns.[20]

In spite of the improvement of its defences, however, Portsmouth's
relative decline as a naval port continued. Not only Deptford but the
new and rising dockyard and base at Chatham almost entirely supplanted
it. The change from France to Spain as England's main enemy, and
Spain's possession of the Netherlands which so closely confronted the
waterway to London, provided a powerful additional reason why the
Thames yards were given priority. No warships were built at Portsmouth
during Elizabeth's reign, nor in those of her first two Stuart successors
James I and Charles I; neither did ships of war usually lie there, the
customary station for those not in commission being Deptford or
Woolwich.[21] Another serious fire in 1576 which nearly destroyed the
dockyard was a further reason for the prolonged period of relative
obscurity through which the town was now passing.[22] Even its share in
the defeat of the Spanish Armada was small. Three of the Queen's ships
seem to have been fitted out there before joining Drake in January 1588
when he called in on his way from the Thames to Plymouth; and when
the beacons of the Isle of Wight gave warning of the Armada's coming
the men of Hampshire mustered behind its ramparts. Several noblemen
and gentlemen went out to join the English fleet; victuals and powder
which had been sent down were put on board the fleet as it passed by in
its battle with the Spaniards; and four small ships were provisioned and
sent out by the lord lieutenant of the county, though too late to be of any
service. One was a Lowestoft vessel; the others may have been Portsmouth ships, though it is not so stated.[23] But the gunfire died away
up-Channel and presently the men who had been mustered went to
their homes again in peace.

Within the town the reign saw two events which were both important
in widely different ways; one tragic, the other spelling civic progress.
The first, in 1563, was a terrible visitation of the plague such as most
towns suffered from time to time in that age, though not always so
severely, and of which the Great Plague of Charles II's day was the last
and (except for the Black Death) the worst example. A presentment of
the Court leet jury only three months before the outbreak gives some
idea of the conditions which bred these calamities, here and elsewhere:–

There was given in pain [under penalty of a fine] of twelve pence the
peace [order] to every inhabitant that the common gutter and other

gutters in the town should be kept clean and scoured every week the Friday night . . . This order is not kept, but certain sweep it down before their neighbours' doors and so let it be, and some carry away nothing at all, and other wash their buckings [foul underclothes] at the wells whereby they greatly annoy the rest of the town, wherefore there is now given in pain of 3s. 4d. the peace that none wash any more bucks at the well, nor leave any filth before their neighbours' doors . . . and that the butchers make clean the places of the market from time to time weekly where they sell the flesh in pain of every offence twelve pence.

The jury also made presentment of some owners of property 'against the churchyard' because there was not only stench but also filth of water and such like to the annoyance of people that pass by'. When it is added that in a seaport the indigenous rats which throve on such filth would be joined by others that found their way ashore and brought a variety of germs with them, it is hardly surprising that the plague is said to have carried off a third of the population* in a few months; especially since escape to the country was not only forbidden in order to prevent the pestilence from spreading but could in practice be prevented much more completely in an island town like Portsmouth than elsewhere. Trade came to a standstill; frightened people either betook themselves to prayer-meetings (though compulsory church-going had been suspended) or went furtively to astrologers and soothsayers for prophecies or charms; and burials were carried out hastily and at night by men who were brave or drunk, or both. Yet through it all the civic authorities and a number of apothecaries and nurses stuck to their posts until with the coming of the winter the plague died away.[24] Since there had also been another disastrous fire in 1576 it is hardly to be wondered at that a petition for government aid in 1585 lamented 'the great ruin and decay of the town'.[25]

A happier event was the grant by the Queen of the town's first charter of incorporation in 1600. Until then it had been practically governed by the charters of Richard I and John, which had been confirmed on a number of occasions. Elizabeth's grant, after reciting the ancient constitution and privileges of the borough and referring to the ambiguities of these earlier documents and to its important position, declared that its inhabitants should henceforth be a body corporate under the title of the Mayor and Burgesses of Portsmouth, with the usual corporate legal personality, involving the right to acquire lands and privileges, plead and be impleaded, and possess a common seal. It also declared that the Mayor during his year of office and three of the senior burgesses were to be justices of the peace, and went on to recount the functions of the other officers of the corporation. Important as the

---

* It is impossible to give an accurate estimate of the population of Portsmouth at this time, since most of the town's registers for this period have been lost; but the number of permanent residents has been put at under 1000 and the plague caused 300 deaths.

charter was, much of its importance lay in its being a formal and legal recognition of existing facts.[26]

A development which foreshadowed some of the troubles of the next century, though perhaps rather faintly, was the growing animosity between the townsfolk and the garrison. As early as 1547 the then Captain of Portsmouth (the title of Governor was not yet being used) had laid a complaint against the Mayor about the gauging of beer; and between 1559 and 1564 so much discord developed between the Corporation and the Governor, Sir Adrian Poynings, that the Mayor made a formal complaint to the Lord Treasurer, alleging that the Governor had released criminals arrested by the constables, one of whom had been savagely assaulted by his retainers and imprisoned in his house overnight. He had also caused some of the town's officers to be put in the stocks and the Mayor himself had been insulted by one of his servants, who had made 'a flip with his finger and thumb, saying "tushe" for him with many unseemly and noisome words'.

In spite of this complaint, bad relations continued during the governorship of the Earl of Sussex (1571–93), who made the townsmen cut down the hedges near the walls and whose successor they welcomed with a blunt statement that now they had 'some hope to grow rich, which heretofore was impossible by reason of the great dislike between them and the dead Earl'.[27] The increase of this animosity during the next two reigns helps to explain why the garrison, with a hostile population behind it, was only able to make a feeble defence during the short siege at the beginning of the Civil War.

At this stage it may be well to summarize the main features of Portsmouth and Portsea Island as they were about the end of the sixteenth century. On the seaward side the town's defences, looking up-harbour from its entrance, consisted of the rampart known as the Long Curtain, the Great Platform, the Square and the Round Towers with the wall between them where the Eighteen-Gun Battery was later to develop, while on the landward site it was encircled by earthworks. Its street plan, as illustration no. 4 shows, was basically the same as it is to-day. From the Landport Gate on the north side of the town ran the road to London, and the other gates were the Quay Gate which gave on to the Camber and Point Gate opening on to that peninsula through the recently-built wall mentioned above. Point itself was as yet undeveloped, for the Elizabethan map shows only two houses there; and its notoriety as a sink of iniquity lay in the future.

Immediately north of the fortified town stretched the Mill Pond. A little to the north of this again the still very small dockyard was situated by the harbour shore, while inland of it and also to the north of the Mill Pond was land known as the Common. Beyond this and on either side of the London road lay several town fields divided into furlongs and strips allocated to various inhabitants. Elsewhere there were scattered villages, hamlets and farms. The southern part of the island, the site of the modern seaside resort of Southsea, was a waste of marsh and common, some of it below sea-level and subject to inundations from the sea, with Southsea Castle standing on its southernmost tip.

The island of Portsea was divided among three parishes—Portsmouth (coinciding roughly with the town), Portsea (which covered by far the greater part of the island) and Wymering. This last parish was largely on the mainland, where the village of that name was situated, but extended over the northern part of the island and took in the hamlet of Hilsea. In the late seventeenth or early eighteenth century also, a tidal marshy bay on the east side of the island was drained and became an extra-parochial area called Great Salterns because of the salt-extracting works there. This area remained Crown property until 1830. The whole of the parish of Portsmouth and part of that of Portsea were included within the boundaries of the borough, which extended far beyond the fortified town, while the parts of the island outside these boundaries were under the jurisdiction of the county magistrates.[28]

4. For King or Parliament? 1603–1660

Under James I Portsmouth's decline from the promising developments of a century earlier reached its lowest point. The peace made with Spain within a year of the King's accession put an end to the privateering in which the seamen and merchants of the town had taken part and from which they had made some profit. Such work as the dockyard had lately had shrank again. The Navy was neglected and allowed to fall to a level unknown since the days of Henry VI. In 1623 Henry VII's dock was filled in with rubble to prevent it from being eroded by the sea and was not replaced for thirty years, during which time the vested interests of officials, officers and shipwrights whose convenience and financial advantage were bound up with the yards on the Thames and Medway stood in the way of any revival of Portsmouth's; though a more respectable reason for the maintenance of their primacy was that for fifteen years after 1630 the presence of timber-worm in the harbour was suspected. The yard now consisted mainly of storehouses and there was still no permanent force of shipwrights; parties from other yards took duty there in turns, until after a master shipwright had been stationed permanently at Portsmouth in 1638 a body of shipwrights was established there in 1645.[1]

Nevertheless under Charles I there was a steady increase in the use made of the port.[2] At first this owed a good deal to the King's favourite, George Villiers, Duke of Buckingham, who had been made Lord High Admiral and took his office seriously. Before Charles's accession his father had hoped to marry him to the King of Spain's eldest daughter, in pursuit of a pipe-dream James had had of playing peacemaker between the mutually hostile Protestant and Catholic camps in Europe; and Buckingham had carried the Prince off on a romantic but ridiculous secret journey to Madrid to woo her personally. The escapade ended in a humiliating fiasco, but the news that the prince was not after all going to marry a 'Popish' bride was greeted with great joy by all good Protestants, including the people of Portsmouth, who gave Charles and Buckingham an enthusiastic welcome when they landed there on their return. When he became king Charles reciprocated by making a gift to the town of a bust of himself, which was erected on the Square Tower (where it still is) in 1635, with the following inscription:

'After his travels through all France into Spain and having passed very many dangers both by sea and land he arrived here the 5th. day of Octocer 1623. There was the greatest applause of joy for his saftey through the kingdom that was ever known or heard of'.

But by this time Charles's arbitrary actions after his accession were causing growing discontent, and this was made worse locally when the then Governor of Portsmouth, Lord Wimbledon, provocatively ordered the men of the town to give proof of their loyalty by doffing their hats when passing the bust. It is therefore hardly surprising that the second sentence of the inscription was erased after the outbreak of the Civil War.[3]

Nevertheless one outcome of the warm welcome Portsmouth had given the two returning adventurers was that the town had had an opportunity of pointing out its decline to Buckingham and he had lent a sympathetic ear.[4] However before he had been able to do much for the town and port he had wanted revenge for the rebuff which his un-conventional embassy had received from the Spaniards. Just as he had led Charles into this humiliation, he had then led England into an equally humiliating and unsuccessful war with Spain which had opened with the miserable failure of an attack on Cadiz in 1625. One of the few people to emerge with any credit from this ill-led and ill-found venture (which sailed from Plymouth), however, was a Captain John Mason, who was about to become a prominent citizen of Ports-mouth and whose destiny was to be tragically linked with Buckingham's.

Son of a merchant of King's Lynn, Mason was already a sea-captain trading to Amsterdam and elsewhere when at the age of twenty-four he somehow caught the eye of James I and was appointed to command an expedition against a rebellion in the Hebrides. Success in this brought him friends and further fortune. He spent six years as governor of a small colony in Newfoundland, exploring the neighbouring lands and developing what became his highest ambition, to found more colonies overseas and build a new world in America; an ambition which he partly—but only very partly—realised by acquiring grants of land and establishing in later life one of the first settlements in what came to be called New Hampshire. Before this, however, he had returned to England in 1621, and four years later, thanks to the fortunate circum-stance that his cousin Robert was Buckingham's secretary and on excellent terms with the Duke, he was appointed commissary-general to the Cadiz expedition. For the shortages of food and drink that marred this ill-starred enterprise no blame was imputed to him, however, and on the contrary he won commendation as an 'honest, sufficient, careful officer' and further promotion in the new enterprise that Buckingham had lost no time in launching in order to retrieve his credit.

This was an operation against France aimed at relieving the Protestant Huguenot seaport and stronghold of La Rochelle, which was being besieged by the French king's forces under the personal direction of Cardinal Richelieu. This time it was at Portsmouth that a fleet and an army were assembled, though by hand-to-mouth methods that were little better than before. Mason had now bought the best house in the town, then called the Greyhound but now No. 11 High Street and known as Buckingham House, and as paymaster of this army he struggled against the appalling weaknesses of an administration that voted him large sums but sent him actual cash only in driblets and arrears, expecting officers to provide their men's pay out of their own pockets and innkeepers and householders to maintain free of charge the soldiers billeted on them, until such time—if it ever came—as money might be forthcoming to repay them. Cajoling, coercing, and uttering such warnings to the Privy Council as 'This payment must be made without fail, otherwise mutiny and disbandment will follow', Mason somehow managed to find pay and clothing for the men, get them billeted, and parry in one way or another the protests of their reluctant hosts. But the expedition failed almost as miserably as its predecessor and less than half the troops survived to return broken in health and morale.

Even now Buckingham's only thought was to get together another fleet and army and renew the attempt. He had planned a new dry dock for Portsmouth, but the same continual delays that had prevented its building hamstrung his (or rather, Mason's) preparations for this fresh attack. The men, moreover, had completely lost faith in their rulers and commanders. When the Mayor, the victualler Henry Holt, was ordered to billet sick seamen on shore and found that his fellow-citizens refused to have them because of the disturbances they created and the infection they spread, he put 150 of them in two old houses of his own, for which they requited him by tearing down the walls and lofts, burning fences and casks, and doing (Holt estimated) more than £40 worth of damage. He complained, too, that as a merchant engaged with others such as the Puritan brewer William Haberley in victualling the reassembling fleet he was on the verge of ruin because he could not get paid the £4000 due to him for this and so in his turn could not pay his own creditors. He owed so much money in Southampton and Newport in the Isle of Wight, he declared, that he dared not venture into either town for fear of being set upon. It is evident, however, that there was another side to these complaints, for the wills of both Holt and Haberley show that they had made large fortunes. They were in fact profiteering extensively and investing their profits in real estate. Much of the stores they and others supplied, moreover, were being pilfered by the seamen, who sold them to make up for their unpaid wages. They were deserting wholesale, too, and those who remained were almost uncontrollable.

To this crowded, discontented and insanitary town (where the plague had broken out again in the previous year) came Buckingham in August 1628; a man doomed to a death he more than half foresaw. Warned to wear armour against assassination, he refused; but on taking leave of his royal master he commended his wife and children to Charles's care, saying 'Some adventure may kill me'. As we have said, Mason had by now made Portsmouth his permanent home, buying the best house in the town, today No. 11 High Street and known as Buckingham House because of what was about to happen. The Duke stayed with him (or rather, on him he quartered himself); and when he was leaving the house to attend the King who was with his court at Southwick a few miles away, a throng of 300 seamen surrounded his coach in the High Street and one of them sought to drag him out into the road. Buckingham, who never lacked courage, leapt forth and grappled with the man, and with the help of his escort arrested him. But after his departure for Southwick the man's comrades surged round Mason's house, demanding his release with angry threats to which Mason thought it best to yield. When Buckingham returned from Southwick, however, he happened to meet and recognise his assailant in the street and had him re-arrested, whereupon a mob of furious sailors attacked his guard with stones and cudgels. Officers came running to the rescue from all sides; Buckingham and his attendants put themselves at their head and charged the crowd, laying about them recklessly with their swords, and drove them down to the waterside at Point and so to their ships, though many of them were left lying dead or wounded.

On the day after the arrested man's execution, when Buckingham had breakfasted and submitted his handsome person to the attentions of his barber, he gave audience to a group of Huguenots. Argument rose high about the best method of conducting the proposed new campaign; the Frenchmen gesticulated vehemently, and the Duke prepared to leave for Southwick. As he came forth into the hall he paused to speak with one Sir Thomas Fryer, who was bowing low when a hand shot over his shoulder and a dagger was plunged to the hilt in Buckingham's breast. Plucking it out, the Duke gasped 'Zounds, the villain has killed me!', took a step or two forward partly drawing his sword, fell and died soon after. The hall was too crowded for it to be certain who had struck the blow. Some of the Duke's officers thought one of the Frenchmen must have been responsible and drew upon them, but were restrained by cooler heads. Search was made, and in the kitchen was found a man who made no attempt to defend himself or to escape but stepped forward saying 'I am the man! Here I am!' He was John Felton, a lieutenant in the army whose application for promotion Buckingham had contemptuously rejected and a fanatic who imagined that his deed would be the salvation of his country. After his execution his body was hung in chains on Southsea beach, where the stump of the gibbet long remained. The expedition to relieve La Rochelle then sailed, but too late to be of any use, for the Huguenot stronghold surrendered just as it was arriving.

John Mason continued to handle the financial aftermath of these inglorious enterprises and to live as a prominent citizen of Portsmouth for the rest of his days. In 1634 he became Captain of Southsea Castle, which he considered not only 'the outwork of the town and chief guard of the harbour' but also 'the most exquisite piece of fortification in the kingdom'. Since at this period of his life he was also employed to survey the forts at Gravesend and Tilbury and was then given a commission to travel throughout the kingdom twice a year and report on the state of its defences, he was presumably well qualified to judge. The Castle had fallen into decay of late and had also suffered from a fire in 1626, but Mason 'repaired the walls of the moat and the drawbridge and gates' and planned extensive alterations. He also retained his wider interests, colonial and other, and his contacts with influential London merchants and even with the Court, winning Richard Weston, Lord High Treasurer and afterwards Earl of Portland, as his patron in place of Buckingham. In 1635 he died.

In that same year a visitor to Portsmouth, a trained-band (or militia) lieutenant from Norwich called Hammond, who was clearly a genial soul, left on record a racy and vivid account of his visit, which occurred during a tour of the south of England. Coming from Chichester, he ascended Portsdown Hill, where he 'breathed, and took fresh air both from sea and land'. Then he 'descended down for Portsmouth, and so over a bridge [Portsbridge] some two miles from the town'. Having reached it, he was stopped and cross-questioned by a sentinel at the Landport Gate who had been warned of his approach by a toll of the bell from the watch-tower on top of the steeple of St Thomas's Church.

I told him truly [recounted Hammond] both my quality and that I came from good company, good mirth, good cheer and good wine: all which would not make a good pass, till I further told my intentions; and having done so I told him that I desired to be quartered in a good inn for the time I stay'd, which by his good directions I soon obtained. So on I went as I was directed to my inn, which was the Red Lion. My hostess there was brisk, blythe and merry, a handsome sprightly lass, fit for the company of brave officers . . .

Hammond spent little time in dalliance, however, but went immediately to the Governor's house, where he hoped to find an officer to whom he had a 'pass' (probably a letter of recommendation). This officer was not there, but instead Hammond had the luck to meet an acquaintance from his part of the country, ' an honest blade . . . who was as glad to see me as I was to see him'. The two promptly repaired to the Governor's wine-cellar, accompanied by his chaplain and steward, 'and there nimbly took off two or three hearty glasses of excellent choice wine', which enabled Hammond 'the better to march the rounds' with his friend and visit his quarters. They then 'mounted the walls (where no stranger is admitted to pass without his guard)' and watched two warships leave harbour, dipping their topsails in salute to Southsea Castle and firing six guns, to which the fort replied with three. Then after he had 'marched the rounds, quartered the streets and offered up devotions at God's House in their fair chapel there', he departed for the Isle of Wight in a boat which he had engaged, without returning to the Red Lion, since the wind was getting up and the boatmen were 'calling earnestly on [him] to hasten away'. Indeed, he and they found 'the blustering winds and rolling waves so unfit for that passage at that time' that all were seasick and he had to be put ashore at Hill Head and make his way on foot to Titchfield, where he spent the night.[5]

Neither the fortifications which Hammond saw nor Mason's repair of Southsea Castle, however, prevented the latter from playing a rather ignominious part, or the town from making only a poor defence, in the siege of Portsmouth at the beginning of the Civil War in 1642. Indeed, the war might almost be said to have broken out at Portsmouth, since that place saw what was probably the most important of the local conflicts with which the struggle began. Both sides were anxious to secure the chief naval ports; and since Parliament held London and the south-east and had thus deprived the King of the Thames with its commercial and naval facilities Charles hoped that if he could secure Portsmouth he would have a stronghold in the south and a sallyport through which he could bring the men and supplies he hoped for from abroad. But since the Navy had declared for Parliament this would be difficult at best, and even if he did win Portsmouth its usefulness to him would be limited—a consideration that probably weighed with the townsfolk, who must have reflected that a Royalist occupation of the town would mean the loss or serious decline of its main source of employment and prosperity. Practical self-interest must thus have reinforced the resentment which many of them felt at royal exactions and the arbitrary acts of the King, his ministers and officers.

Which side the town would take, however, depended in the first place mainly on the Governor, Colonel George Goring, a dissolute, erratic, but in some ways gifted soldier who had gained experience and a reputation in the Thirty Years War—a man more capable of sudden action in an emergency than of steady and sustained effort. Originally reckoned by the Royalists a staunch supporter, he had gone over to Parliament but secretly continued in communication with the King, and three weeks before Charles set up his standard at Nottingham he executed a second *volte-face* and announced that he would hold Portsmouth for his sovereign. But his preparations for a siege proved altogether inadequate; supplies were short and the defences imperfectly repaired; most of his troops (about 300 in number, many of them pressed men) were far from enthusiastic and desertions were frequent; so that he made but a feeble defence. A superior Parliamentarian force under Sir William Waller, who was afterwards one of the leading generals of the early part of the war, was assembled on Portsdown Hill and in the neighbouring mainland villages; but not much is known about its composition except that it included trained bands from Hampshire, Sussex and Surrey, a Scottish contingent and two troops of horse. Ships were brought up to blockade the port; and the only naval vessel Goring had, the *Henrietta Maria* (named after Charles's queen), was captured and carried off up Fareham Creek in a brilliant little cutting-out operation under cover of darkness. Next the Royalist outposts were driven from Portsbridge, where 'a little fort or bulwark of earth' had recently been built, and compelled to fall back within the town ramparts. Before this reverse, however, hundreds of cattle, sheep and pigs had been commandeered by Goring's men from the fields and villages which still covered the bulk of the island and their unfortunate owners had been forced to drive them into Portsmouth to be slaughtered and salted down. The Royalist soldiers also plundered the farms and cottages of all 'corn, meal, flour, beef, bacon, bread, butter, cheese, eggs and all their poultry and ducks, . . . to the great terror of all the people, especially women and children, forcing poor and rich to come away and beg for bread to keep them alive'. A number of the country folk, however, were rescued by a landing force from the blockading ships and many of the women and children among them were conveyed across Langstone Harbour to safety on Hayling Island.

After a series of not very bloody skirmishes outside the town walls and a characteristically daring but unsuccessful attempt by Goring to beat up the Royalist camp by night, the next stage in the siege began when the Parliamentarians built works at what was then the little fishing village of Gosport and mounted guns on them in order to bombard the town from across the harbour. On September 2 they opened fire, their shot reaching as far as the Town Mount near the Landport Gate and causing much alarm. Next day they turned their attention to the tower of St Thomas's Church which the garrison had been using as a lookout, and laid both it and the nave in ruins that were not repaired until after the Restoration of Charles II. Another target that same morning was the town mill, a direct hit being scored on the bed of the miller, who luckily for himself was an early riser thanks to the exigencies of his calling and who ever afterwards 'commended it for a good thing to rise betimes in the morning'.

Under cover of this bombardment preparations were made for an attack on Southsea Castle, whose defenders had shrunk by now to a mere dozen, probably through desertion. However this intention was detected and the captain in command, a local man named Challoner, went into the town to confer with Goring, whom he found either unwilling or unable to send reinforcements from his now depleted force. The two apparently spent as much time in carousing as in conferring, and when an inebriated Challoner wove his way back to the Castle he promptly went to bed and to sleep. Later that night an overwhelming Parliamentary storming party, more than 400 strong, advanced with scaling-ladders to assault the fort. A feint attack was also made on the far side of the town, but Goring was not deceived and his gunners opened fire on the true attackers. These, however, got under cover on the seaward side of the Castle, which for its part could do them little harm, not only because of the paucity of its defenders but because most of its guns had been transferred to meet attack from the landward side. A parley now took place with the sleepy and still muzzy-headed Challoner, whose first reaction was to complain of the unreasonable hours chosen by the besiegers for battle and to suggest thay they should all wait till morning and discuss the matter then. But the Parliamentarians, losing patience and evidently thinking that they would be better sheltered from Goring's guns—still firing furiously—if they were inside the Castle, proceeded to storm the walls without meeting any opposition, whereupon Challoner hastily surrendered and 'promptly fell to drinking of the King's and Parliament's health in sack' with the officers of the storming party.

This easy capture of the fort, whose cannon were now turned on the town, destroyed what little was left of the morale of the dwindling garrison. The Mayor of Portsmouth and several officers escaped over the wall and most of the men threw down their arms in spite of Goring's appeals to them to hold out a little longer, 'being possessed with fear of having the town battered down on all sides and being frighted more by their wives'. Only about sixty of the defenders, nearly all 'gentlemen and their servants which were not used either to traversing of great guns or use of muskets', were willing to fight on. Recognising the hopelessness of the situation, Goring therefore capitulated, though by threatening to blow up the magazines to the great damage of the town he secured good terms. The remnant still faithful to him were allowed to ride out with the honours of war, taking their arms and personal possessions with them, while he himself took ship to Holland. From there he soon returned to play a not undistinguished part on the Royalist side in the war, his most striking achievement being to put to flight nearly half the Parliamentarian army at Marston Moor and almost win that battle in spite of Fairfax and Cromwell. For the rest of the war Portsmouth remained firmly in Parliament's hands; though near the end, when the Royalist cause was virtually lost, Goring made a brief reappearance with a small force, intending to lay siege to Portsea Island from the landward side. Finding it too strongly fortified and garrisoned, however, he gave up all hope of belatedly turning the tables and withdrew.[6]

During what is called the Second Civil War in 1648, when the seizure of power by Cromwell and the army provoked many former Parliamentarians and most of the Navy to change sides, giving the Royalists new hope, the eight ships lying at Portsmouth remained steadfast in their allegiance; and afterwards the Parliamentary garrison petitioned for the trial of the King, though their pay was still in arrears thanks to the cost of the war to their party.[7]

The eleven years of the Commonwealth period which followed the execution of Charles in 1649 saw the second and more lasting rise of

Portsmouth as a dockyard town and naval base. The grimly competent group of Puritan republicans who now ruled England were not men to let grass grow under their feet. Only a few days after the King's death Colonel William Willoughby, who before the war had been a timber merchant and had then engaged in salvage work in the Thames, was appointed Navy Commissioner at Portsmouth. Other commissioners were sent to the Thames yards, and Willoughby was ordered to hasten to his post and get ships to sea to clear the Channel of pirates and Royalist vessels. This he was evidently quick to do, for (having also been made a commissioner—or justice—of the peace for Hampshire) he soon had several pirates lodged in the county gaol. For two years he worked tirelessly; in fact, by early in 1651 he had worked himself to death in his efforts to carry out the flow of instructions that poured in on him. Under him the dockyard hummed with activity, and naval shipbuilding began again after more than a hundred years during which no warship had been built there. First came the 38-gun *Portsmouth*, launched in 1650 and followed by a dozen more vessels under the Commonwealth, eleven of them in the next six years. Apparently the pace also killed Willoughby's successor, Captain Robert Moulton, within twelve months, and in turn he was succeeded by Willoughby's son Francis, who was evidently quite as much a glutton for work as his father had been—which was fortunate, since the outbreak of the First Dutch War (1652–4) soon after his appointment made his labours all the more urgent.[8]

This war hastened the rise of Portsmouth, though for the time being and for geographical reasons it was Chatham which benefited most from it and saw its lead increased. Nevertheless during the struggle Portsmouth played a considerable part as a victualling centre and building and repair yard, as well as serving conveniently for the receipt of wounded and prisoners after Blake's hard-won victory off Portland and the Isle of Wight in 1653. The prisoners were distributed between Portsmouth, Gosport, Cowes, Southampton and Winchester; but the sick and wounded were naturally assigned to the first three of these places, as being the nearest. They were quartered mostly in private houses, taverns and beershops, which last were complained of as small and stifling, besides exposing their occupants to the temptations of drink. One of the surgeons who attended them was more sweeping and general in his denunciation of 'the filthy nastiness' of Portsmouth, 'unpaved, undrained, and enduring an epidemic of smallpox', but the surgeons themselves received the praise of the Navy Commissioners for taking good care of the men. Among the wounded was Blake himself, who had been hit in the thigh by a splinter and took a long time to recover, since his general health was poor at the time.[9]

During the war Commissioner Willoughby had discussed with the generals-at-sea the possibility of enlarging and improving the dockyard, and had written to the Admiralty Committee of the Council of State recommending the purchase of five acres of neighbouring ground for building storehouses and a ropewalk and laying timber. The Committee did not accept the whole of this proposal, but agreed to the leasing of an acre and a half, which enabled Willoughby to build two ropewalks. The war had also convinced him of the difficulty of getting the work of the yard done without a dry dock, and in 1655 he complained to this effect. After some delay partly due to labour troubles which included a shipwrights' strike, a new dock which would take third- and fourth-rate ships was completed in 1658. The war was now over, but Willoughby's efforts and the labours of the dockyard could not be relaxed. He continued his exertions to get the ships that were on the stocks finished, and searched far and near for timber, especially in Carisbrooke Park in the Isle of Wight and Bere and Arundel Forests on the mainland, for he was anxious to kill the idea that Portsmouth was an expensive yard; indeed he claimed that it could build ships twenty per cent more cheaply than other places. He also searched and agitated for more workmen, for the town had not yet a resident artisan population equal to the demands that were now being made on it. But gradually men began to settle down in the neighbourhood of the yard and came to expect permanent employment; their sons became apprentices; a dockyard community grew up; and though impressment had still occasionally to be resorted to, voluntary engagement became the rule. The steady growth of the demand for labour was creating the supply. The first move to provide houses for dockyard officers inside the yard, too, had been made when one was built for the Master Attendant in 1654.[10]

In the events which led to the restoration of Charles II after Cromwell's death Portsmouth played an important part. After Cromwell's feeble son Richard had faded from the scene, power at first rested with the army, or rather the handful of leading generals known as the Wallingford House group. To clothe their naked sword-rule in some rags of constitutionalism they recalled that 'Rump' of the Long Parliament which had presided over the first four years of the Commonwealth until it was kicked out by Cromwell. But soon a clash occurred between the generals and the rather doctrinaire republicans headed by Sir Arthur Hesilrige, Sir Henry Vane and Edmund Ludlow who dominated the Rump. The issue was whether the sword or the civil power which the Rump claimed to represent should be the real ruler; and since the army had force at its command it expelled the Rump again.

At that point Hesilrige decided to meet force with force in order to restore parliamentary rule once more.[11] A Leicestershire gentleman who had been prominent in opposition to Charles I before the war, he had fought in it with some distinction, raising and leading a regiment of cavalry who from their heavy armour were nicknamed 'the Lobsters', and becoming second-in-command to Sir William Waller in his west-country campaigns. He had friends who were also experienced soldiers and he and they knew that by no means all the army was solidly behind the generals. In particular the garrison of Portsmouth under the Governor, Colonel Nathaniel Whetham, sympathised strongly with the twice-ejected Rump. The town or at least the leading townsfolk were staunchly parliamentarian, and Hesilrige knew that Admiral Lawson's fleet was prepared to come over to him. He therefore resolved to secure Portsmouth and make it the centre for gathering forces to march on London and restore the Rump again in the name of parliamentary republicanism.

In December 1659, then, he rode into Portsmouth with his friends Colonel Morley and Colonel Valentine Walton and established himself at the Red Lion, where they were speedily joined by Colonel Whetham. A rapid and bloodless *coup d'état* followed. The few officers of the garrison who were not of their way of thinking were seized and imprisoned; and next morning the civic authorities gave in their adhesion, headed by the Mayor, John Tippetts, who was also the Master Shipwright. Other leading citizens who accompanied him included Josiah Child, a London merchant who had come to Portsmouth in 1655 as victualler and deputy treasurer of the fleet and had already been Tippetts's predecessor as mayor; Richard Lardner, a member of a well-established local family, who owned wharves and storehouses at Point; and Francis Holt, one of the sons to whom the brewer and victualler Henry Holt had left the considerable properties he had amassed by supplying fleets and armies during Buckingham's expeditions. Like them, most of the little group of well-to-do merchants who governed the town's affairs were either dockyard officials or made their living by supplying the forces with provisions or equipment. Hugh Salesbury and St John Steventon were Clerk of the Survey and Clerk of the Cheque* respectively; Francis Holt's brother John was like him an alderman; Nicholas Peirson was a wealthy shipowner who possessed considerable property at Point; and Nicholas Hedger was a rising brewer and mercer. All these were Parliamentarians and most or all were Puritans who on the Sabbath day sat under Benjamin Burgess, a Presbyterian who was Vicar of Portsmouth under the Commonwealth

---

* The Clerk of the Survey kept the accounts of the stores from the notes of receipt and issue passed to him by the storekeeper. He also surveyed all ships' stores returned to the yard, and acted as an indirect check on the officers drawing stores.

The Clerk of the Cheque's duty was to muster the dockyard workmen and the companies of the ships in harbour and then make out the paysheets on the basis of these musters and indent for the necessary money. He had also to ensure that his colleagues, the other dockyard officers, did not employ the men for purposes of their own, to countersign all bills that they had already signed, make out the warrants which empowered victuallers to put ships' companies on harbour victuals, and issue imprest bills to the captains. (J. EHRMAN, *The Navy in the War of William III, 1689–1697*, pp. 100–1).

now that the Anglican clergy had been extruded from their pulpits. In their place what may be called a new state church had been set up, representing the leading forms of what had previously been non-conformity, with each congregation provided with a minister conformable to the persuasion that was dominant within it. In Portsmouth those whose political and religious views did not meet with the approval of the group now dominant had been in some cases shut out from citizenship; Anthony Haberley, for instance, another brewer whose family had been prominent in Buckingham's time, had disappeared from the burgess roll after 1650, though he was not among the half-dozen townsmen who were seized and imprisoned along with the dissident officers—presumably because their opposition to the *coup* had been made manifest or was anticipated.

Preparations were at once begun to defend Portsmouth against any move by the army chiefs. Ten warships which were lying in the harbour either defected to Hesilrige or were seized by his supporters; a fort on Portsdown Hill was reinforced with more guns and a garrison; some of the country gentry rode in with armed followings; and Hurst Castle and the Isle of Wight declared for Parliament. A force despatched by the generals to blockade the town changed sides and marched in to join the garrison. Other troops followed, so that Hesilrige soon had command of about 3000 horse and foot; whereupon the Wallingford House ring, uncertain of the loyalty of the forces left to them, made a virtue of necessity, recalled the Rump for the second time, and invited Hesilrige and Morley to come to London. This they did at the head of their troops, gathering more as they went.

Hesilrige now seemed well set for supreme power; but another and more decisive march on London soon followed, for General Monck, the commander in Scotland, now intervened. Leading his army south to the capital while keeping silent about his intentions, he then insisted that the members of the Long (or Civil War) Parliament whose expulsion by the army just before the execution of Charles I had reduced it to the so-called Rump should be reinstated. A result of this was that Hesilrige now lost the majority following he previously had and was thrust into the background. The restored Long Parliament now dissolved itself and a new Convention Parliament was elected which accepted the conciliatory Declaration of Breda that Charles II promptly issued from his exile and welcomed him back. Monck became Duke of Albemarle and Hesilrige was sent to the Tower, where he died a few months later.

Portsmouth's support had enabled Hesilrige to triumph over the generals and that triumph had in turn given Monck the opportunity for which he was waiting. But Hesilrige's victory had been one for continued (though parliamentary) republicanism; Monck's was a victory for monarchy (though on terms). Portsmouth was therefore, in modern colloquial language, out on a limb. The ruling oligarchy did their best to climb down. First they accepted Charles's Restoration with due formality. Then they addressed themselves to the awkward fact that after Hesilrige's successful *coup* honorary burgess-ship had been conferred on him, Walton and another of his allies, Nicholas Love, who had been one of the signatories of Charles I's death-warrant and as such was explicitly excluded from pardon by the Declaration of Breda. It was now conveniently discovered that in the haste of events they had never sworn the usual oaths and they were therefore declared 'expunged out of book'. Another precaution taken was to begin to admit leading members of the opposition or loyalist party in the town to the burgess-ships and even to office from which they had been long excluded. Haberley in particular was readmitted and regained his aldermanry. Not that the exclusion had been complete, for there were some moderates or loyalists among the burgesses and it was one of these, John Timbrell, who became mayor in 1661 in succession to Tippetts's successor Lardner.

In the meantime, while the restored King was feeling his way, retribution tarried. It was nearly a year later before the blow fell. In 1661 the Corporation Act had been passed, restricting municipal office to those who took the sacraments of the Church of England, subscribed to the Oaths of Allegiance and Supremacy, and made a public declaration that it was unlawful to take up arms against the monarch. But it was not this which was used against Portsmouth; or at any rate refusal to take the oaths was not formally advanced as the reason for the drastic purge which presently followed. In the late summer of 1662 five commissioners descended on the town, charged to discover who were fit 'to be entrusted with the carrying on of His Majesty's service and interest in the corporation of Portsmouth' and who should be expelled therefrom because they had been and were 'disaffected to His Majesty'. Tippetts, Child, Lardner, Peirson, Richard Ridge the town chamberlain, Hedger and Colonel Whetham (who had already lost his Governorship in 1660) headed the latter list, which was remarkably long—97 persons in all, as against 40 expulsions at Leicester, 39 at Chester and 13 at Exeter. Benjamin Burgess and other Puritan ministers were at the same time driven out from the pulpits they had lately occupied.

Surprisingly the Holts escaped almost completely, the only member of the family to be ejected from the Corporation being one (Thomas) who was also a Puritan parson. Francis even retained his aldermanry, though his brother John prudently resigned from his. On the other hand there was promotion for loyalists and those who could at least rank as such by virtue of not having compromised themselves deeply with Hesilrige, as well as for some newcomers. Haberley was recommended as the next mayor; Steventon and three others, two of whom had come to the town only in 1660 and 1661 respectively, were given the alder-manries vacated by the leading expellees; and John Timbrell Junior was made chamberlain in place of Ridge. As Miss Dorothy Dymond writes, 'the whole character of the town and its government must have been turned upside down by this sweeping, drastic, wholesale change of personnel'.

The loyalist group remained in power, or at least in office, during the first part of what for them were 'good King Charles's golden days'. Tippetts, however, was indispensable as a very able master shipwright at a time of naval expansion, and no less a person than the King's brother James Duke of York, who had become Lord High Admiral, interceded for him to retain his post. He became a commissioner of the Navy in 1668, surveyor in 1672, and was knighted in 1675; and since he probably had no strong political views and cared chiefly for his professional career it is unlikely that he regretted very much his exclusion from further civic honours. Josiah Child went back to London to play a big part on a very much wider stage as the panjandrum of the East India Company, of which he became a director and eventually Governor. He too was knighted, in 1678, published a *New Discourse of Trade* in 1693 in which he argued for freer commerce and which has caused some to regard him as an anticipator of Adam Smith. He died worth £200,000, a vast sum then. The lesser figures among the disfranchised stayed in Portsmouth, where some of them paid repeated fines for following their former callings while they were no longer freemen of the town. But even if they paid these fines for the rest of their lives the sums involved were not ruinous, and in due course several of them worked their passages back to burgess-ship and office. Peirson, for instance, was constable in 1665, alderman in 1670 and mayor in 1672; Hedger was re-elected alderman and mayor in 1673; and Ridge alderman in 1682 and mayor in 1684. In other cases where the head of a family had, like Lardner, been too deeply committed with Hesilrige to recover, a younger member was allowed to make a come-back. On the religious side the Toleration Act of 1689 which followed William III's accession enabled Presbyterianism to emerge again into the full light of day with the establishment of a chapel in Penny Street in 1691.* In these ways some of the beliefs and principles of the Puritan Parliamentarians of the Civil War and Commonwealth survived with modifications, to reappear as the dominant Whiggism of the town in a later age.

---

* The first minister known to have served the congregation which established this chapel was John Hickes, who when a fugitive after Monmouth's rebellion was given shelter at Winchester by the aged Lady Lisle, for which she was condemned to death by the infamous Judge Jeffreys.

5. The rise to primacy as a naval port

The leaders of the loyalist party in Portsmouth pursued during their dominance a policy of strengthening themselves by prevailing on great men and officials connected with the Court and the Navy to accept honorary burgess-ships. An early and minor example was Samuel Pepys the diarist, who was Clerk of the Acts (i.e. Secretary) to the Admiralty. Of his first visit to the town, accompanied by his wife, in 1661, before the purge had placed the loyalists in office, he had written that Portsmouth seemed

a very pleasant and strong place. And we lay at the Red Lion, where Haslerigg [sic] and ... Walton did hold their council when they were here ... Several officers of the Yard came to see us to-night; and merry we were, but troubled to have no better lodgings.

May 2. Up: and... to walk round the town upon the walls. Then to our inn; and there all the officers of the Yard to see me with great respect and I walked with them to the Dock and saw all the stores... Back, and brought them all to dinner with me and treated them handsomely; and so after dinner by water* to the Yard, and there we made the sale of the old provisions... And so to the town again by water;* and then to see the room where the Duke of Buckingham was killed by Felton...

May 3. Early to walk with Mr Creed† up and down the town; and it was in his and some others' thoughts to have got me made free of the town; but the Mayor [Lardner] was it seems unwilling, and so they could not do it.

When he came again without his wife in April 1662 Timbrell was mayor and things were different. After he had finished his business in the dockyard,

... after dinner, comes Mr. Stephenton [Steventon], one of the burgesses of the town, to tell me that the Mayor and burgesses did desire my acceptance of a burgess-ship and were ready at the Mayor's to make me one. So I went and there they were all ready and did with much civility

---

* The town and the yard were of course separated by the inland stretch of the Mill Pond, though Pepys had evidently walked round it in the morning.

† John Creed, Deputy Treasurer of the Fleet, who had travelled down with Pepys.

give me my oath; and after the oath did by custom shake me all by the hand. So I took them to a tavern and made them drink; and paying the reckoning, went away... It cost me a piece in gold to the Town Clerk and 10s. to the bailiffs, and spent 6s.[1]

During the early part of Charles II's reign the dockyard continued to be improved, a good deal of extra land being won from the harbour mud for new buildings. Nevertheless naval business and administration were often ill conducted, and went on being so well into the eighteenth century. Labour and stores were freely used by officials for their private ends; the seamen and the soldiers of the garrison remained unpaid for weeks; and tradesmen, especially bakers, often became bankrupt because of the large sums owed them by the Admiralty. Sudden shortages were liable to be caused when suppliers refused to furnish any more provisions until the Victualling Department settled long-standing obligations. Ropemakers, sawyers and other workmen repeatedly grew mutinous because their wages were not paid, and left without notice to seek work elsewhere. In 1665 the Comptroller wrote urgently for money to stop 'the bawlings and impatience of these people, especially of their wives, whose tongues are as foul as the daughters of Billingsgate'; and Colonel Thomas Middleton, who had succeeded Francis Willoughby as Commissioner in the previous year, had to lend the men ten shillings apiece to prevent a mutiny. This proved vain, however, since a fortnight later mutiny did break out, whereupon the exasperated Commissioner 'seized a good cudgel and took more pains in the use of it than in any business during the last twelve months'. 'He has not been troubled since', it was reported. Nevertheless he had another problem, that of finding suitable accommodation for himself and his family, which comprised nine children and twenty-six persons in all, according to a letter he wrote to his friend Pepys; though by the current use of 'family' this number would include servants and perhaps even some subordinates. 'Where I am now', he declared, 'we are forced to pack nine people in a room to sleep in'. Pepys at once authorised him to build himself a Commissioner's House in the dockyard.[2]

Middleton's troubles must have been further increased, however, by the renewal of war with the Dutch in 1665 and the fact that soon after it began the plague came again to Portsmouth. Afterwards known as the Great Plague, it had begun in London, and when it was known that the King and his court were thinking of evacuating themselves to Portsmouth the townspeople naturally feared that they would bring it with them. Prayers were offered up and pesthouses built to isolate any sufferers, but these spiritual and material precautions proved vain, for though the Court ended by going to Salisbury the plague came by sea, as so often before. When a ship which had it on board entered the harbour some of the crew hurried ashore before they could be stopped and at once spread the infection. Soon people were dying at the rate of fifteen a day, but mercifully the outbreak was relatively short and came to a sudden stop.[3]

Though Portsmouth had no intimate share in either this Second Dutch War in 1665–7 or the Third in 1672–4, since they were fought in the North Sea, the renewed growth of Anglo-Dutch hostility for some time beforehand set on foot a reorganisation of the town's defences. To undertake this Sir Bernard de Gomme was commissioned in 1665. He was himself a (Flemish) Netherlander, but had served the Royalists with marked ability during the Civil War and had now been made Engineer-in-Chief of the King's Castles in England and Wales. His work, on which Dutch prisoners of war were employed, went on for more than twenty years, transformed the fortifications, and was not finished until after both he and the King had died in 1685. Like the great Vauban in France and the leading Dutch military engineers, he was primarily concerned to increase the depth of the fortifications by means of additional water barriers together with outworks in and beyond the moats. Leaving the original line of the town ramparts unchanged, he remodelled the ramparts themselves and in particular the bastions, widened the moat and constructed a second moat outside it and separated from it by a continuous narrow 'island'. On the counter-scarp or outward side of each moat there was a glacis, that is, a con-tinuous earthwork sloping at such an angle as to deflect shot over the ramparts. The inner face of each glacis was vertical, so that each protected a covered way between it and the moat behind it, thus providing advanced positions for cannon and musketry fire and assembly points from which the defenders could launch a sally. At the Landport De Gomme built a ravelin (a detached bastion forming a triangular island in the moat) which had the result that anyone approaching the town on the road from Portsbridge had to cross three bridges, across the outer moat, across the inner moat to the ravelin, and from the ravelin to the gate, respectively. A modification which he began before the works were finished was to break up the 'island' or strip between the two moats to form four large ravelins, each centrally positioned before a length of the curtain wall. This, however, was not completed until the middle of the eighteenth century. On the seafront he constructed the Spur Redoubt in front of the Long Curtain* and remodelled the Ten-Gun Battery (to the east of the Square Tower), which had originally been built in the previous century. Further into the harbour mouth and abutting on the Round Tower, the Eighteen-Gun Battery also came into existence in the last phase of his reconstructions. Guns had first been mounted there about 1540, but whereas the works were originally merely of timber De Gomme rebuilt them in stone with eighteen casemates rather shallower than those of to-day.[4]

---

* The Long Curtain, running between the Saluting Platform and Clarence Pier, is the only part of De Gomme's main scheme of defences surviving in something like its original condition.

Another of the last and partly posthumous phases of his work was the construction of King James's Gate, named after Charles's brother and successor James II, to replace Point Gate in the wall that stretched across what later came to be called Broad Street and faced towards Point. On this little peninsula many houses had been built and streets laid out during the seventeenth century, so that it had become quite a populous area; but it was still left outside the town's defences, which were strengthened here by cutting a moat from the Camber to the harbour on the outer or Point side of the wall. Point was thus exluded from the town more emphatically than before, and so came to be regarded as being to a great extent outside its law. Among the many privileges it enjoyed which were denied to residents within the town itself was the right of licensed victuallers to keep their houses open both day and night. Hence it won an evil reputation for drunkenness, disorder and immorality. The first house built on it in Elizabeth's reign had been a drink-shop, and by 1716 there were forty-one beerhouses, sleezy coffee-houses and brandy-shops, besides the numerous brothels. Notorious for brawls and tumults, it was sometimes said—though no doubt with some exaggeration—to be the wickedest place in Europe.[5]

When De Gomme's fortifications were finished Portsmouth was one of the most strongly defended towns in England, since in addition to its walls, bastions, counterscarps, ravelins and moats the Mill Pond made its northern defences almost inaccessible and the 'Little Morass' on the near side of Southsea Common would have made an attack from the south-east very difficult. Furthermore he had remodelled and improved the defences of Southsea Castle and surrounded the dockyard, which still lay apart from the fortified town, with an earthen rampart topped by a strong wooden palisade. Gosport, too, which was now growing in importance, had been fortified by a rampart and moat on its landward side, while a battery corresponding to the Eighteen-Gun Battery on the Portsmouth shore of the harbour entrance had been built on Blockhouse Point facing it. This was the nucleus of the later Fort Blockhouse.

Meanwhile James II, in pursuit of his design to make Roman Catholicism once more the dominant religion of the country, was seeking to place Catholics and other supporters in key positions and to make sure of the armed forces and strong places of the kingdom. In this policy Portsmouth naturally occupied an important place, and James dismissed the Governor, the Earl of Gainsborough, who was also Lord Lieutenant of Hampshire and Ranger of the New Forest, to make room for his own illegitimate son the Duke of Berwick in all three capacities. He had also been filling up the army with Irish Catholic soldiers, a body of whom he sent to the town to be mustered into the Eighth Foot, who were stationed there and of which Berwick was Colonel-in-Chief. The lieutenant-colonel, John Beaumont, and five of his captains promptly protested against these recruits as not only Papists but little better than barbarous savages, declaring that if more men were needed they would have no difficulty in enlisting sufficient Englishmen, and offering to resign their commissions. They were not allowed to do this, however, but were court-martialled and cashiered. Their stand was applauded throughout the country and the case of the 'six Portsmouth Captains' paralleled at the time the better-known trial of the Seven Bishops for protesting against the Declaration of Indulgence by which James on his own authority granted Catholics liberty of worship and freedom to hold public office.[7] Both acts of defiance (the latter by the applause with which the main body of the army, encamped on Hounslow Heath, greeted the news of the bishops' acquittal) should have served to warn James that he could not rely on the army to back him.

James's expulsion by the Glorious Revolution of 1688, his flight to take refuge with his cousin Louis XIV of France who was the champion of the Catholic cause in Europe, and the accession of William of Orange and his wife Mary Stuart to the English throne brought about a reversal of English foreign policy which was of vital importance to Portsmouth. A generation and more of enmity towards Holland gave place to an alliance of the two countries based on common Protestantism and common interests against France, which once again became England's main enemy, as she had been for much of the Middle Ages. A long series of wars began between them—seven major struggles stretching between 1688 and 1815 at intervals that were mostly brief—which have been collectively called the Second Hundred Years War. And this meant that whereas Chatham's geographical position had made it the country's chief naval base while the Dutch (and before them the Spaniards in the Netherlands) were the enemy, the same dictates of geography rapidly brought Portsmouth—facing France as it did—to the premier place by the end of the century.

Already by the time of the Third Dutch War, halfway through Charles II's reign—the busiest years the dockyard had yet known—it stood second only to Chatham's, and by the close of the reign it had overhauled Chatham in the construction of large warships, though the latter was launching a greater aggregate tonnage.[8] There was still only one dry dock, however; but in 1691 a new one and two wet docks were begun, and in the next ten years they were completed on a large area of land which had been reclaimed and enclosed to the north of the existing dock; an extension which doubled the size of the yard. Then in 1701 another, the North Dock, was built further north again; and in 1703 yet another, the South Dock, was added. In 1704 more large sums were voted for new storehouses, a wharf and a boundary wall to replace the 'Pallisadoes', as De Gomme's earthwork and wall were called. This high brick wall, which included a new main entrance to the dockyard that was henceforth known as the Main Gate, was completed in 1711.*

---

* A section of this wall still forms part of the boundary of the dock-yard on its southern and south-eastern sides, and other stretches are preserved within the yard.

These works at first contributed to the overtaking of Chatham and then latterly were tokens of it.[9]

Another development traceable to the war with France that had been sparked off by William's accession was the conversion of a building at the north end of St Mary's Street, which had originally been erected as a hospital, into the Colewort Barracks—the first barracks within the town for troops, who had hitherto been housed in the towers and gates of the fortifications.[10]

The street pattern of the town in the seventeenth century (basically the same as in the sixteenth) shows three parallel main thoroughfares, High Street with St Thomas's Street on one side and Great Penny Street on the other, running from north-east to south-west; then St Nicholas or Little Penny Street parallel to Great Penny Street on the south-east and High Market (later Warblington) Street parallel to St Thomas's Street on the north-west. The continuation of High Street along the Point pensinsula became known in due course as Broad Street; and St Mary's Street ran south from the northern angle of the fortifications. The population increased after the revival of the dockyard under the Commonwealth, despite bad sanitary conditions and frequent outbreaks of disease. The mercantile trade of the harbour, however, declined as the naval development progressed, and in 1676 there were only eleven vessels belonging to the port, the largest being merely of seventy tons burthen. The customs receipts were therefore very small.[11] But whereas at first the town had had comparatively little to do with the dockyard lying then half-a-mile north of it, and had not been very much influenced by it, from the middle of the seventeenth century the two began to react on and contribute to the growth of each other, with dockyard officials holding municipal offices and leading merchants supplying the yard with provisions and equipment.

The whole town had formerly lain within the narrow limits of its fortifications. But as the dockyard and its labour force grew, houses began to spring up to the northward on what was then known as the Common but was later to be called Portsea. The first of these, known as the New Buildings, were erected partly on ground reclaimed from the mudlands of the harbour which formed a salient projecting into the dockyard that was conveniently situated for the employees of the yard who lived in them to enter it by what was then the North Gate. A Governor at the turn of the century, Colonel John Gibson, however, complained forcibly that they obstructed the field of fire from the ramparts, pointed out that regulations forbade any dockyard workmen or other townsfolk to live outside the defences, and threatened to blow the offending dwellings to pieces with his guns. Luckily Queen Anne's amiable consort, Prince George of Denmark, was easily prevailed on to intervene during a visit to the town; Gibson was overruled, and the new suburb, or satellite town as it became, was free to grow. Nevertheless even well over a century later some low-built houses in what was then

Portsea were still called 'garrison houses' because, it was said, their original builders had not dared or been allowed to build them any higher lest they should interfere with the outlook from the fortifications,

Colonel Gibson, who was clearly a choleric man, suffered another frustration at the time of Anne's death in 1714, this time in common with all those Jacobites like himself who were hoping that when this happened James II's son the Old Pretender would be able to return from exile as her successor. A plot was being formed by one of her leading ministers, Henry St John, Lord Bolingbroke, to bring this about or at least to seize power and dictate the succession. Since the plans involved control of key posts and places, it is possible that the Jacobite Governor of Portsmouth may have been privy to them. But the steps the conspirators proposed to take were still incomplete when Anne died so suddenly that they did not venture on any action. The news of her death was brought to Portsmouth by a nonconformist townsman named John Carter, who was naturally a strong partisan of the Hanoverian succession—the succession, that is, of the Elector George of Hanover (the future George I), who was both a Protestant and a descendant of the House of Stuart through the female line. Carter, whose descendants were to play a big part in the town's history, had happened to be in London at the time and at once set out for Portsmouth where, although he made the journey on foot and took three days, he arrived before the next stage-coach.* But the irascible Gibson, who may have been expecting to receive further instructions from Bolingbroke or other directors of the conspiracy the moment the Queen died, refused to believe him and immediately clapped him into gaol as a seditious rumour-monger; though he was forced to release him when the coach arrived with confirmation and doubtless the news that George I had already been proclaimed king. Legend has it that the anti-Jacobite majority of the townsfolk, in order to take a rise out of the discomfited supporters of the Pretender, immediately began to ask them, 'Do you know Queen Anne is dead?' and that this was the origin of the long-surviving sneer sometimes cast in those words at purveyors of stale information or people who did not seem aware of what was going on around them.[13]†

---

* There is nothing incredible about this. Coaches travelled only at a walking pace over the bad roads of those days, and Carter, who presumably had a start, was a robust man in the prime of life who would be making the best speed he could.

† A flood of light has been cast on the life and administration of the town during the period covered by this and the two following chapters by the publication, since this book was written, of the admirably produced first two volumes of the Portsmouth Record Series, which contain an abundance of illuminating documents.

6. Progress and peril

The eighteenth century saw Portsmouth established as the heart and centre of British sea-power. Almost every one of the great naval expeditions that went out to victory in this era sailed from there. Rooke to the taking of Gibraltar, the elder Byng to Cape Passaro, Vernon to the capture of Portobello, Rodney to the Battle of the Saints, Howe to the Glorious First of June, all set out from Portsmouth. To it Anson returned in the *Centurion* with a quarter of a crew and half a million pounds from a four years' voyage round the world; and from victory on the waters and shores of the St Lawrence came a fleet with flags half-mast, bearing the body of James Wolfe to burial with his ancestors.

It was not always victory. On a stormy day in March 1757 a great crowd gathered on the ramparts and along the shore to see an admiral shot 'to encourage the rest', as Voltaire said—John Byng, a younger son of the victor of Cape Passaro, guilty not of cowardice (for he was a brave man) but of an error of judgement which had led to the loss of Minorca. Under the harsh law of that day the penalty for what proved literally a fatal error could be death. An incompetent ministry, panic-stricken at the disastrous opening stages of the Seven Years War, which was nevertheless to end gloriously, leapt at the chance of making him a scapegoat. George II refused to grant a pardon; and Byng, who comported himself with the utmost dignity and courage, was shot on the quarterdeck of the *Monarque* at Spithead.

But after all, the consequences of Byng's mistake, though serious, did not come within many hundred miles of touching Portsmouth directly. Twenty-two years later, during the American War of Independence, danger threatened it to the heart; nothing less than capture and possible retention by the French with the aid of their Spanish allies.[1] 'Never at any other time in history', a French naval historian has written of this episode, 'not even when Napoleon's army lay encamped at Boulogne, was the French navy so near its oft-dreamt-of goal, the invasion of England'; and his judgement has been endorsed by the sober estimate of his British counterpart Professor Christopher Lloyd that 'at no moment since the Dutch were in the Medway was the country's peril so great'.[2]

59

For in Napoleon's day the Fleet blockaded his ports of departure and virtually the whole of Britain's defence forces were within our island; whereas in 1779 most of our regular army and a good part of our navy were 3,000 miles away across the Atlantic struggling to subdue the American rebels, while an enemy fleet in greatly superior numbers not only entered the Channel but seemed to command it.

Napoleon's great invasion plan was in fact no more than the last of a long series of such projects formed in France during a century and a half, which are still preserved in the French naval and military archives at the Chateau de Vincennes in Paris. Among them lies a map of eighteenth-century Portsmouth, significantly tattered and much fingered. For in this long chain of projects the idea of striking at Portsmouth and the Isle of Wight had often figured. After the Seven Years War had ended in a resounding defeat of France this invasion-planning took on a new spirit of bitterness and desire for revenge, and the wish to destroy the root of British naval strength by capturing our principal naval base developed more strongly and positively than before. When Britain's quarrel with her American colonies showed signs of escalating into a war that would give France her opportunity of vengeance the output of such invasion plans grew. Hitherto they had usually envisaged an attack on Portsmouth from inland, after a landing further along the coast to the eastward, and had regarded the capture of the Isle of Wight as a minor and rather incidental accompaniment or sequel. But it happened that at this time Cherbourg was being developed as a naval port in order to give France a base in the Channel confronting Portsmouth,* and as a result the concept of an attack on the great British stronghold became one of direct assault from the sea, with the seizure of the Isle of Wight a necessary preliminary or at least a much more important part of the operation.

France's entry into the war in support of the Americans in 1778 was therefore followed early in the next year by a secret agreement with Spain (which as her ally in the latter part of the Seven Years War had also suffered defeats at Britain's hands and thirsted equally for revenge) to join her and co-operate in an attack on Portsmouth and the Wight. It was calculated accurately that the British would have about 35 of the line or a few more available in the Channel and that a combined Franco-Spanish fleet of 50 (in the end it numbered 66) would suffice to beat them if they fought or blockade them in their harbours if they refused battle. Once control of the Channel had been secured by one means or the other, light vessels would be despatched to Havre and St Malo to escort the transports which would bring over 30,000 picked troops.

The French at once took steps to obtain the full, first-hand and

---

* Eastward of Brest the French had previously had no harbour for heavy ships which could compare with Portsmouth or Plymouth, but only ports which could take a comparatively few small craft.

up-to-date information about the town and neighbourhood that would be necessary, by sending a trusty and daring officer to reconnoitre—a Major Berthois de la Rousselière, who had previous experience of intelligence work in British ports. With one companion whose identity remains unknown but who may have been one of the handful of obscure and venal British traitors who were in French pay at this time, La Rousselière performed a prodigy of espionage. Having made their way to London, the pair disguised themselves as British seamen, La Rousselière as a cover for (presumably) speaking with a French accent perhaps posing as a Channel Islander, of whom there would be a number on the lower decks of the Navy and whose first language would be French. They then travelled down to Portsmouth, where they evidently received some local help, perhaps from one or more of the aforesaid type of traitor-agent.* Having made, as La Rousselière reported afterwards, 'several tours of the fortifications on the outside and of a great part on the inside', they crossed the harbour to Gosport twice, obtained a boat and in it examined Spithead, where the Channel Fleet was lying at anchor, as well as St Helen's Roads, the Needles Channel and the coast of the Isle of Wight from Cowes to Yarmouth. They then landed in the island and inspected part of the interior on foot, after which they returned to London and La Rousselière to France. Both on entering and leaving Portsea Island they took note of what were then called the Portsea Lines, a continuous rampart across the north shore of Portsea Island between Portsmouth and Langstone Harbours which was in fact the first form of what were afterwards called the Hilsea Lines. The Lines were not occupied, however, 'no doubt because of the shortage of troops', since the two spies reported the entire garrison of Portsmouth as consisting only of one battalion of militia and some companies of invalids (old or partly disabled soldiers who were considered still fit for garrison duty though not for service in the field). The fortifications of the town itself seemed to the professional eye of La Rousselière (who was an engineer officer) to be in excellent order, but Gosport was 'virtually without defence, protected on the landward side only by an ill-maintained entrenchment'.

The plan of attack which the allied enemy formed was that when the British fleet had been got out of the way, by battle or a diversion, the Isle of Wight should be taken. The main attack on it was to go round the east of the island and through Spithead, though a feint might be made through the Needles Channel. A landing, for which not more than 4,000 men would be needed since the garrison was scanty and scattered, would be made on both sides of the Cowes river and the troops would march at once upon Newport, after the fall of which there should be little or no

---

* Possibly from David Tyne, a Scotsman employed in Portsmouth Navy office, who was executed in 1782 for traitorous correspondence with France (GATES, pp. 460–1).

further resistance in the island. All should be over in a single day. Next, simultaneous attacks were to be made on Gosport and Portsea Island after relays of warships had beaten down the fire of Southsea Castle, Lumps Fort and Fort Cumberland,* which defended the shore facing Spithead. Gosport must be assaulted by a force of 6,000 or 8,000 landed in Southampton Water under the warships' protection. When it had been taken the dockyard and lower town of Portsmouth could be bombarded from across the harbour. Meanwhile, starting two hours before dawn, 20,000 men in four waves would attack Portsea Island itself. The right wing of the first wave, 3,500 strong, must penetrate in small boats into the channel between it and the neighbouring island of Hayling, braving the fire of Fort Cumberland and then landing beyond it and pressing northward to take the Portsea Lines in the rear. The centre and left wave would land on Eastney and Southsea beaches respectively, the task of the centre being to contain Southsea Castle, while the left wing cut the communications between it and the town. At the same time 4,000 of the force which had taken Gosport would launch an attack across the harbour, cut the communications between the town and the dockyard, and march to aid the division attacking the Lines or create some diversion to help it. As the other waves of the main body came in from the Isle of Wight the siege of the town would be formed, which it was reckoned would be over in a week. All the troops left in England would no doubt be concentrated in an attempt to relieve or retake the place but their efforts would be frustrated by putting a sufficient force into the Portsea Lines, which could not be turned without local command of the sea. Portsmouth could then be either held permanently as a sort of French Gibraltar or perhaps exchanged for that place in the treaty of peace (which would be a spur to the Spaniards to do their utmost).

At this time not only was Britain without allies but the Navy was so divided by political dissension that it proved impossible to find an admiral of real ability willing to take the command of the Channel Fleet, and it devolved upon the elderly, amiable but ultra-cautious Sir Charles Hardy. The commander-in-chief of the Army, Lord Amherst, was also past his never very brilliant best and was moreover convinced that the enemy intended to attack London, for which reason he insisted on retaining in Kent and Essex the bulk of the 20,000 regulars left in the country. In addition there were about 30,000 militia, mostly raw or at best half-trained, of whom Portsmouth had as its garrison three regiments now (with a fourth at Gosport) and six

---

* Both Lumps Battery, facing on to Eastney beach, and Fort Cumberland, as yet only a small stone-built structure constructed in the extreme south-east of Portsea Island in 1746 to prevent waterborne forces entering Langstone Harbour, were parts of the same scheme of strengthening the defences to which the Portsea Lines belonged. See below, p. 69.

companies of invalids, but no regulars at all except a few artillerymen; totalling about 2,600 men altogether. On the other hand the newly-appointed Governor, Lieutenant-General Sir Robert Monckton, who had been Wolfe's second-in-command at Quebec at the age of thirty-three and so was by no means an old man twenty years later, was calm, competent and completely imperturbable.

For the defence of the Channel it was at first only with great difficulty that thirty ships of the line, with a due proportion of frigates and other smaller craft, could be mustered; and Hardy sailed with these from Spithead, much too late to prevent the French from leaving Brest for their rendezvous with the Spaniards off Corunna. But the Spanish fleet from Cadiz was slower still, and by the time it had reached the rendezvous seven weeks late disease which was probably typhoid fever had broken out in the French ships. Even then another week was spent in co-ordinating signals, and it was more than a fortnight after that again before the combined fleet appeared off Plymouth, where (since it was not known that it had no troops on board) it caused something of a panic exodus among the civilian population. From Plymouth the news and something of the alarm passed rapidly from port to port along the Channel and soon reached Portsmouth, which many correctly guessed would be the object of the attack. Here again civilians began to flee inland, while the garrison made their preparations under Monckton's watchful eye and a boom was laid across the entrance to the harbour. To complicate things further, Hardy, whose force had meanwhile been increased by ones and twos to 38 of the line, had struggled down-Channel against contrary winds and passed the enemy without either fleet being aware of the other's presence. When this became known both put about and in the foggy weather then prevailing passed each other again unknowingly. Only after that did they sight each other, whereupon Hardy withdrew up-Channel with the enemy at first in pursuit, his declared object being to lure them on as far as he could into waters increasingly unfamiliar to them, further and further from Brest and nearer to his own ports and possible reinforcements. But even when the enemy were no longer in sight he continued on his course and reached Spithead unmolested, where he might have been blockaded in if they had been able to continue the pursuit. Unknown to him, however, when he first sighted them they were already at the end of their tether and practically powerless. Sickness had continued to run rife through French and Spanish vessels alike, and in the French ships, which had been longer at sea, water and provisions were beginning to run short. They were therefore compelled to turn and put into Brest, where the French alone disembarked more than 8,000 sick. How many the Spaniards put ashore and how many dead had been cast into the sea are not known. All idea of a descent on Portsmouth or any other part of England had to be given up for that year, and by the next the two Bourbon Powers had decided to concentrate instead on sending men and ships to aid the Americans.

Portsmouth had been saved from capture (though it is unlikely that the enemy could have held it for very long), not by Admiral Hardy or General Monckton—gallant fight though the latter would doubtless have made with his pitifully inadequate forces—but by Providence and pestilence.

Throughout these wars and rumours of wars (and thanks to them) the expansion of the dockyard continued. In 1717 the line of officers' houses called the Parade was built, and in 1723 twenty-seven more acres were added to the yard, which was spreading steadily to the northward. Brick replaced timber as the material of which its buildings were constructed and in 1764 the Lords of the Admiralty visited it and laid down the outline of a plan of orderly development, including an additional dry dock. By 1775, according to the *Guide to Portsmouth* published in that year, the dockyard 'resembled a town in the number of its dwelling-houses, offices, storehouses, lofts and other edifices. . . . It contained amazing quantities of everything necessary for the Royal Navy. There were never less than two thousand men employed in it, and in times of war upwards of 2500'. In the remaining quarter of the century, during which more new docks, workshops and stores were built, the number of men employed grew to over 4,000.[3]

This state of affairs was reached in spite of disastrous fires in 1760, when the earlier wooden ropehouses were destroyed and afterwards replaced by new ones with brick walls and internal timber framing; 1770, when these in turn were destroyed; and 1776, when their successors were set on fire though not gutted.[4] This last fire was the work of a mentally unbalanced social misfit named James Hill, *alias* Hinde and Aitken, but much better known posthumously by his nickname of 'Jack the Painter'. He had originally followed this trade before taking to a wandering life of crime, committing highway robberies, burglaries and rapes, and then fleeing overseas to the American colonies to escape arrest. Here he had imbibed the view of Britain as a cruel and bloody tyrant which was current among the rebellious extremists with whom he seems to have consorted, and he presently returned with a wild plan of setting fire to her naval dockyards, shipping and even her principal cities. Having made a tour of the dockyards of southern England, which he found almost completely lacking in security precautions and thus wide open to espionage (as De la Rousselière's exploit a little later showed) he took lodgings in Portsmouth and prepared to begin operations. Having managed after one failure to lay and ignite a trail of gunpowder in a ropehouse, he panicked and fled forthwith not only from the yard but from the town. Nevertheless the fire he had kindled did some damage, though it fell short of his full intention. Tracked down, he was tried and hanged on the mainmast of the famous frigate *Arethusa* (which had been set up in the dockyard as a gibbet), professing repentance and recommending the authorities to exercise 'great care and strict vigilance' at the dockyards in future—which they did not do, however. His bones hung bleaching on the gibbet for many years until, as the story goes, some sailors took them down and used them to pay an alehouse debt.[5]

Even greater changes took place in the dockyard after Brigadier-General Sir Samuel Bentham, the brother of the jurist and political theorist Jeremy Bentham, became Inspector-General of Naval Works in 1795. Originally apprenticed to a shipwright, he had become a naval architect and engineer and had executed several major engineering works in the Russia of Catherine the Great. Besides completing or carrying out some important operations in the dockyard, including the construction of a large basin and several dry docks, he introduced many improvements in dockyard machinery and shipbuilding. In particular he collaborated with the eminent civil engineer Marc Isambard Brunel (whose even more distinguished son Isambard Kingdom was born in Portsea in 1806) in developing machinery to revolutionise the manufacture of wooden purchase blocks, which were then a basic requirement for the Navy. The blockmaking factory which the elder Brunel established in the yard continued in operation for more than a hundred years, with only the source of power changing.[6]

An anonymous but admiring visitor to the dockyard in 1807, after describing this 'wonderful block manufactory, where machinery of the most ingenious invention peforms every operation but that of the last polish', went on to record that the heat of the anchor-forge, into which he passed next, was so intense that the men who worked there had to be supplied with eight and a half pints of beer a day. This, with wages of twenty-nine shillings a week, sufficed to tempt 'these Cyclops to abridge their lives and live in this emblem of Tartarus for sixteen hours every day.'[7]

Meanwhile the decline in the relative importance of Chatham and the Thames dockyards, though gradual, had continued in the eighteenth century; but in the second half of it the Plymouth (or rather, Devonport) yard, which had been relatively unimportant a hundred years earlier, grew to a size comparable with Portsmouth's. In a report of Admiralty inspections in 1771 the merits of the two ports as naval bases were compared. Plymouth, it was concluded, had the depth of water for laying up more large ships; and since its situation made it the readier outlet into the Atlantic, commanding the entrance to the Channel and immediately opposite Brest,* it was the best port for cruising squadrons. But the intricate convolutions of the entrance to its harbour made getting ships in and out more hazardous than at Portsmouth, and for want of a spacious safe roadstead like Spithead it could never be the main rendezvous for the great fleets in time of war. Plymouth Sound

---

* It should be remembered that this report was written just before the French began to develop Cherbourg.

was not safe for large ships to lie except in summer, and even then not for very many vessels, because of the limited space of clear ground. Should the British fleet be defeated in a great sea-battle, too, the place would be exposed to a sudden attack, not being as defensible as Portsmouth. The latter, moreover, was better placed for timber supply, with the New Forest and those of Bere, Waltham and the Weald at its command—though Plymouth had the Forest of Dean.[8]

The growth of Portsmouth's dockyard naturally meant the growth of the town, and since it was closely constricted within its fortifications this growth mainly took the form of the development of the Common into a virtually separate township. From the earliest years of the century houses had begun to be built there outside the walls and north of the Mill Pond, as well as on the East and West Dock Fields further north again. This area developed very rapidly, as the 1775 *Guide to Portsmouth* which has already been quoted recorded:

About eighty years ago this was a common field with only one hovel upon it. But the prodigious resort of people to this port within these years rendering it necessary to increase their buildings, they employed this field for that purpose and have continued to build with such rapidity that from a barren desolated heath it is now become a very populous genteel town, exceeding Portsmouth itself in the number of its inhabitants and edifices.

Populated (despite the *Guide*) chiefly by dockyard workers and keepers of taverns, shops and brothels that catered for the Navy, it continued to be called Portsmouth Common until 1792, when it formally took the name of Portsea. Meanwhile in the 1770s it had been enclosed by fortifications in its turn—a new line of ramparts which ran from the north-eastern part of the existing town walls right round both it and the dockyard on their landward sides to the harbour shore beyond the yard. These new defences were mainly on the same principles as De Gomme's, but on a larger scale and with some refinements of detail.[9] Towards the end of the century, therefore, the same process of overspill began to repeat itself and yet another settlement, largely working-class and mainly along the line of the present Commercial Road, began to grow up in its turn outside these newer walls. Commencing with a handful of dwellings called the Halfway Houses because they were halfway between Portsea and the village of Kingston, this was afterwards named Landport after the Landport Gate.[10]

With most of the urban development thus taking place outside the walls of the old town of Portsmouth, its street-plan remained essentially the same as it had been for two centuries, with its three main thoroughfares running from north-east to south-west and its two principal cross-streets at right angles to them. Some notable buildings, however, made their appearance during the century. A new town hall replaced in 1739 that built in Henry VIII's day; standing, however, like its predecessor in the middle of the High Street.[11] A grammar school was opened in Penny Street in 1750, thanks to the generosity of Dr William Smith, who had been mayor of the town in 1713 and at his death many years later left an endowment of land in the Isle of Wight to the Dean and Canons of Christ Church, Oxford, for the purpose.[12] A naval academy was set up in the dockyard in 1733, with the object of providing a suitable education for 'sons of the Nobility and Gentry' who were to become officers in the Navy. Hitherto the usual method of entry* for youthful aspirants to the quarter-deck had been the rough-and-ready one by which a lad was taken on board a ship by the captain (who might be, and very often was, his father, some other relative or a friend of the family, or be anxious to oblige the lad's patron if the latter was influential). He then began to learn his profession in the hard way by going to sea at once, after which if he was satisfactory he was in due course made midshipman. This way of entry resembled the apprenticeship system then current in many other callings. On the face of things the Admiralty's object in creating the College was to introduce some initial training and even initial education into the officer ranks. But the late Professor Michael Lewis has suggested that its real motive was a feeling that since these scions of the nobility and gentry had so much 'interest' or pull that they were bound to be the rulers of the Navy when they grew up, it was advisable to try to ensure that they were a little better trained to its ways beforehand than were their lowlier brethren.

The Academy was not a great success, however, The 'College Volunteers', as they were called when they left and were appointed to ships, were unpopular with the captains who had to accept them, perhaps when they wanted their places for their own or their friends' relatives, and who were very possibly inclined to doubt whether book-learning of any sort was useful to sea-officers. The Academites themselves generally disliked the institution because in their eyes it resembled a school and the life they led there was not nearly as free as that which they could have led if they had gone straight to a ship. Bored and restless, they did little or no work, often behaved in a disorderly manner, drank, engaged in precocious dissipation, and in general gave the Academy a bad reputation. It is therefore small wonder that many parents fought shy of it, so that even the limited numbers necessary to fill it were seldom if ever forthcoming. By 1773 it contained only fifteen 'sons of Nobility and Gentry', so that the Admiralty was obliged to ordain that in future fifteen of its places should be filled by 'sons of officers'. At the same time, after an inspection by George III, its name became the *Royal* Naval Academy. But still it did not fill, until with the coming of the Revolutionary (1793-1802) and Napoleonic (1803-15) Wars—the greatest of the 'Great French Wars'—the demand for

---

* I omit the very small percentage of 'Admiralty Nominations', or 'King's Letter Boys', for whom see MICHAEL LEWIS, *A Social History of the British Navy, 1793—1815*, p. 143.

officer-recruits rose to its peak and the Academy's numbers shot up, first to eighty and then to a hundred. Its buildings were enlarged in 1806; its syllabus was modernised; it received an excellent new head-master in James Inman, who was a noted expert in ship-construction, gunnery and mathematics; and its name was changed again to the Royal Naval College. It continued to train cadets until 1837, when it was closed.[13]

By or before the middle of the eighteenth century a theatre had come into being in the High Street, though the exact date of its appearance is uncertain and it is very possible that it or a predecessor may have existed earlier. The first reference to it mentions a visit by a troupe of London actors, but a few years later it was a company from Plymouth (known as 'the Brandy Company' from the nature and frequency of their potations) who were occupying it regularly for a season every summer. Then in 1761, in response to a demand from local gentry and officers of the garrison for a better building and standard of acting, another theatre was built further along the street, where the Grammar School now stands, by John Arthur of the Bath Company. This company now entered into successful rivalry with the Plymouth players, who continued for a time to make periodical appearances at the old theatre, though with poor equipment and a bad reputation, until they and it apparently faded out. Next one Samuel Johnson, who had begun to build a circuit in Wiltshire, Hampshire and West Sussex, is first recorded in 1767 as bringing his company to the newer theatre at Portsmouth. They visited it again in 1769, by which time Johnson had taken into partnership John Collins, who in the later years of the century was to become the dominant figure in the local theatrical world. To-gether they conducted the Salisbury, Winchester, Southampton, Portsmouth and Chichester theatres, though not always all at the same time. Even when they were all under their management only one was normally open at a time and their company toured round for a season at each, Portsmouth's turn coming in the winter and early spring. Until 1788 theatrical performances were actually illegal under an obsolete law, except where an expensive royal patent* had been obtained; and they resorted in their advertisements, as other managers did elsewhere, to such legal fictions as describing the plays they performed as 'lectures' and the theatre itself as a 'histrionic academy'. Collins later took one Davies as his partner and their partnership was said to have made the fortunes of them both.[14]

In 1754, in response to the vogue of sea-bathing and (for a short time) drinking sea-water which developed in the earlier eighteenth century, a bathing-house was built by public subscription in what accordingly came to be called Bath Square, near Point, It was positioned over the water and underneath a trapdoor in the main room was a bath which filled

---

* It was this granting of royal patents to certain theatres which led ultimately to the common name 'Theatre Royal'.

with the tide, allowing secluded indoor sea-bathing. Later it was taken over by the Quebec Hotel next door, which became a rendezvous for passengers to and from the East and West Indies and North America. Known consequently as Quebec House, it ceased to be a hostelry during the latter half of the nineteenth century, but still exists, probably the sole survivor of the wooden-framed buildings which were fairly common in this area of the town during that century.

The first newspaper printed in the town, the *Portsmouth and Gosport Gazette*, made its appearance in 1747 but was discontinued about 1790, when the *Portsmouth Gazette* was established and continued until about 1800, giving place in turn to the *Portsmouth* (later *Hampshire*) *Telegraph*, which had been commenced in 1799 and still survives under the latter name.[16]

The early history of local banking is rather vaguer and more complicated. The first clearly known opening date for a bank is given on a poster announcing the commencement of one by Grant and Burbey at 46 High Street on 25 October 1787. This continued until 1814 at this address, and afterwards throughout the nineteenth century with various amalgamations, finally being taken over by Lloyd's. In November 1787, however, Messrs. Griffiths, Chaldicott and Drew had replaced one Joseph Mounsher as occupants of 92 High Street and were operating as bankers. Whether they had previously been so and whether Mounsher had also been a banker beforehand both seem unclear, but a year later he reappears, apparently as a partner in the firm, for the space of one year. Meanwhile by September 1788 they had moved along the street to No. 59, which had been occupied by a Captain F. J. Hartwell for the previous two years and was referred to as a bank in a poor rate book of February 1788, though the form of the entry suggests that this may only have been because Griffiths, Chaldicott and Drew had already acquired the premises and were about to transfer their business thither. Changes of partners then occurred until this bank became Godwin & Co. in 1809; in 1818 it was dissolved, after which the premises were taken over by Messrs. Grant.[17]

Improvements were also made to the fortifications of the old town during the first half of the century, but by 1750 these had assumed the form they were to retain until the end of their life as a coherent system more than a hundred years afterwards. During the 1740s, while Britain was fighting France in the War of the Austrian Succession, the outlying defences of Portsea Island were likewise strengthened, as has already been mentioned.* Fort Cumberland, Lumps Battery and the Portsea Lines were built at this time, and the pre-existing fort at Portsbridge was reconstructed as part of the same scheme. Gosport, which had a much slower growth than either Portsmouth or Portsea, did not begin to feel the constraint of its walls until the second half of

* See p. 62 above.

the century, but in 1797 they were extended to bring in a new victualling yard; and Fort Monckton was built between 1782 and 1795 on the southernmost promontory of that side of the harbour to match Southsea Castle on the Portsmouth side.[18]

Over the rest of Portsea Island outside the town small villages and hamlets were slowly developing. The largest of these was Kingston at the junction of two of the three main north-south roads of the island, where the road to Fratton branched off from that to Portsmouth and the Common. Along the former a broken line of settlement stretched from St Mary's Church to Kingston Farm.[19] St Mary's, the earliest of the island's churches, had been its parish church since the Middle Ages (while St Thomas's became that of Portsmouth) and was the only one outside the walls of the old town until the eighteenth century. Then in 1704 a chapel dedicated to St Anne was built in the dockyard, and when it was demolished to enable a new house for the Commissioner (which later became Admiralty House, the residence of the Commander-in-Chief) to be erected in 1784 it was replaced in the following year by the present St Anne's Church. Meanwhile in 1752 the Corporation had given a grant of land on the Common for the building of what was to be St George's Church, in response to an appeal from a number of devout dockyard artisans living there, who represented that the walk of about two miles to St Mary's bore hard on them and made attendance impossible for the aged and infirm of the district. Not only did these enthusiasts (in the eighteenth-century sense) contribute to the building costs, but they also undertook to 'buy' the pews when the church was finished in order to provide for its upkeep.[20] There continued, however, to be only the two parishes of Portsmouth and Portsea, the latter comprising all the rest of the island except Wymering parish's bridge-head at Hilsea and the extra-parochial fragment in the east. At Hilsea, between which and Kingston lay the settlement of North End on the London road, this last was joined by the third north-south artery (if a mere lane can be dignified by that name), leading to the villages of Copnor and Milton and extending beyond them to Eastney Farm and one or two small cottages[21].

Methodism seems, rather incongruously, to have come to Portsmouth at about the same time as the theatre. A group belonging to the Countess of Huntingdon's Connexion was in existence in 1750, but it had little influence on the subsequent Methodism of the town. In 1753 John Wesley came to it for the first time and recorded in his *Journal* that he 'was surprised to find so little fruit here, after so much preaching'. 'That accursed itch of disputing', he went on, 'had well-nigh destroyed all the seed which had been sown'. But he returned twenty-one times in the next thirty-seven years and in 1785 he commented: 'After all the stumbling-blocks which have been thrown in the way, God will have many souls in this place'. Among the minor stumbling-blocks may have been the four presumably ill-disposed or hostile individuals who in 1772 were prosecuted for coming among and disturbing the worshipping congregation of the Bishop Street meeting-house in Portsea by 'talking aloud, making a loud noise with their feet, laughing aloud and behaving in a very indecent and irreverent manner'. In 1790, the year of Wesley's last visit, Portsmouth became a separate circuit, having previously been in the Sarum (Salisbury) Circuit.[22]

Two philanthropic figures were produced by the town in the eighteenth century, Jonas Hanway and John Pounds, though the former's activities and the stage on which they were carried out were vastly greater than the latter's—national as opposed to local. The one is commemorated by a monument in Westminster Abbey; the other by a little church in Portsmouth High Street.

Hanway was born in 1712 in Portsmouth, where his father was Agent Victualler for the Navy, but left the town while still young after his father's death. Becoming a merchant and partner of an English trader in Russia, he travelled down the Volga and by the Caspian Sea to Persia with a caravan of woollen goods and returned by the same route after perilous adventures. Having inherited a fortune on the death of a relative, he then returned to England and embarked on his philanthropic career. One of his first acts was to seek protection for children employed as chimney-sweeps. Then in 1756 he became one of the chief founders of the Marine Society, whose object was to recruit men and boys for the sea service and to ensure that they were regularly paid and provided with proper food and clothing. In 1758 he was largely responsible for the inauguration of the Magdalen Charity Hospital, and he also greatly helped the Foundling Hospital in an hour of need. In 1761 he was instrumental in obtaining an act of Parliament —which became known as the 'act for keeping children alive'—making it compulsory for every London parish to keep an accurate register of all pauper children received into and discharged from its poorhouse; and in 1767 he secured another act which made provision for their boarding out not less than three miles from their own parish, at a minimum charge of 2s. 6d. a week with a bonus of 10s. per child per year to each successful nurse. Since these and other activities had left him impoverished, the Government made him a Commissioner for Victualling the Navy—the position his father had held at Portsmouth and which (since he was a man of the most uncompromising honesty) he filled with absolute integrity, never accepting the slightest favour from a contractor or anyone else. Incidently, having discovered the use of an umbrella in Persia, he introduced it into England, patiently enduring and eventually triumphing over the ridicule and insults he received from hackney-coachmen and street-loungers who saw him carrying one around to protect the handsome clothing he habitually wore. Crossed in love in early life, he remained a bachelor and at his death in 1786 left the £2,000 which was all he then possessed to be divided among poor orphans and other needy people.[23]

Eight years earlier John Pounds, a dockyard sawyer's son, had entered the yard as an apprentice shipwright at the age of twelve. When he was fifteen he fell into a dry dock, breaking his thigh and otherwise injuring himself so seriously that he remained a cripple for life, incapable of any but sedentary work. He therefore learnt the trade of a cobbler and after fifteen years of working alone in a little wooden workshop with a living-room above he adopted a one-year-old nephew who had been born crippled. Not only did he manage to cure the child with surgical boots of his own making, but he also taught him reading, writing and botany and gave him religious instruction. In the course of this he discovered that he had a gift for teaching of which he resolved to make fuller use. With hot potatoes and roasted apples as bait he attracted to his workshop thirty or forty other poor and idle children of Highbury Street where he lived and its neighbourhood and set to work to teach them all he knew. He was 52 when he began this philanthropic enterprise and the year was 1818, so that the details of it and its influence must be dealt with in a later chapter.[24]

7. Town government and local politics in the eighteenth century

The government of Portsmouth in the eighteenth century was based on its latest valid charter, granted by Charles I in 1627. In 1683 Charles II, who was then pursuing a policy of packing town corporations in order to use their influence over borough elections to secure a complaisant parliament if he had to call one, had enforced the surrender of this charter and granted a new one framed to serve his turn. But soon after the Revolution of 1688 had expelled his 'Popish' successor James II it had been conveniently discovered that this surrender had never been enrolled and both it and Charles II's charter were therefore treated as void. The 1627 charter which thus remained in force provided for the administration of the town by a mayor, twelve aldermen and an un-specified number of burgesses who varied between the two extremes of 331 in 1681 and 44 a hundred years later. As the latter figure suggests, the Corporation was in practice a close one, in which the aldermen filled up vacancies in their own ranks, appointed the magistrates from among themselves and chose who should be burgesses. These last possessed votes for the members of parliament for the borough and had done so since the Middle Ages, having been confirmed in the possession of the parliamentary franchise by a House of Commons ruling of 1695.* They also took a nominal part in the election of the mayor, though in practice it was the aldermen who controlled the choice of both the latter and the borough members. The government of the town was thus in their hands, which meant that an outstanding personality among them might be able to dominate it.[1]

In the later part of the century the administrative machinery of both Portsmouth and Portsea was reinforced by the creation of what were then called paving or improvement commissioners. Since eighteenth-century corporations were at best slow to realise the need for new or ampler services and sometimes completely blind to it, groups of leading citizens in various towns had begun to apply for acts of parliament granting powers of paving, lighting and watching (i.e., policing) to bodies of trustees who included members of the town council and either

---

* This was not aimed at ensuring it to them, however, but at excluding non-burgesses.

representatives of the ratepayers or persons specifically named with power to fill vacancies. Such applications had become more common in the 1760s, and in 1764 Portsea (or Portsmouth Common, as it was still called) obtained an act appointing such trustees with powers of paving the streets and preventing nuisances. Portsmouth followed suit four years later with an act on a rather larger scale creating commissioners for the better paving, cleansing and widening of the streets and the prevention of nuisances. This act was amended by one of 1776 which made provision also for lighting and watching, and the Common's act was repealed in 1792 and replaced by another which set up a new body of trustees and also bestowed on it its new name of Portsea. In turn this act of 1792 was amended by one of 1827 resembling Portsmouth's of 1776 by making similar provision for lighting and watching.[2]

Meanwhile the Portsmouth commissioners had availed themselves of these acts to improve the police. The number of constables, previously two, had been increased to four in 1652; two for the town itself, one for Kingston and Buckland and one for Point. From 1700 to 1703 there were six constables for the town, but after that the number of officers for the areas outside its walls began to overtake the number of those within them. They were drawn from a wide social range, from the humble artisan to the wealthy tradesman, and a large proportion came from the ranks of the victuallers, who were naturally numerous in a town whose major industry was the supply of the Navy's needs. In 1783 the Portsmouth commissioners decided to reinforce the constables by twelve watchmen who were to patrol the streets at night and whose strength was later increased to twenty. They were ordered to 'prevent all mischief happening from fires as well as all murders, burglaries, robberies and other outrages and disorders, and to arrest and apprehend all Night Walkers, Malefactors and suspected persons who shall be found wandering and misbehaving themselves in any Place'. Persons arrested were taken to the Cage or watch-house on the west side of Point (i.e., King James's) Gate and detained until they could be brought before the justices. Later, instructions were issued that two men were to patrol Point, while two took the north of the town and two the south. They patrolled from eight in the evening until five the next morning, each armed with a staff, and were paid two shillings each per night, being liable to a fine of ten shillings every time they were found neglecting their duty. Carrying rattles to alarm the inhabitants if necessary, they also cried the time of night while on their rounds. Although this old watch system has been much decried, the Portsmouth watchmen seem on the whole to have performed their duties efficiently, with one bad lapse in 1796 when five of them were found asleep in the watch-house while a disturbance was taking place outside. An occurrence in 1817 when one of them, an old man, suddenly fell dead into the arms of the colleague with whom he was going his rounds also suggests that their physical standard may not always have been very high.[3]

Under the acts passed between 1764 and 1792 the commissioners also assumed responsibility for the public water supply. This was obtained from springs either within the town or in the neighbouring common fields, and by now there were public wells or pumps in all the main streets, as well as an unknown number of private ones. But though everybody had access to the common pumps some were not able or willing to collect their water themselves, while others who had their own wells preferred an alternative supply for drinking, and these people were supplied by water-carriers whose prices had been fixed in 1690 at twopence a half-hogshead. In 1694 came the first proposal for a new service, when Richard Barrey of London and George Sorocold of Derby got leave from the Corporation to operate a waterworks, intending to lay on the town's first piped water-supply from springs in White Swan Field opposite the present inn of that name in Commercial Road. Nothing seems to have come of this plan, however. Then in 1741 an act of parliament for supplying the town and its shipping with water was granted to Colonel Thomas Smith, lord of the manor of Farlington, but when he died before he could carry out his project the powers provided by the act passed to his successor Peter Taylor, M.P. for Portsmouth 1774–7, who began by sinking 'an immense well in Crookham Copse near Purbrook and then carrying an archway of brick through Portsdown Hill'. But 'not a drop of water was met with, and the speculation failed'. The town continued to be supplied by the public and private pumps and it was the former of which the improvement commissioners took control.[4]

The strained or hostile relations between the municipal authorities and the military governors and garrison of the town which had existed before the Civil War had long since disappeared; at any rate according to Daniel Defoe, who wrote in his *Journal of a Tour through England and Wales*, published in 1724:

The civil government is no more interrupted by the military than if there was no garrison there, such is the good conduct of the Governors … The inhabitants indeed necessarily submit to such things as are the consequences of a garrison town, such as being examined at the gates… being obliged to keep garrison hours and not be let out [sc., of the town gates] or let in after nine o'clock at night, and the like; but these things no people will count a burthen where they get their bread by the very situation of the place.[5]

Relations with the Navy were a different matter, however. During the first part of the eighteenth century the town was an Admiralty borough; that is, thanks to its dependence on the Navy and the dockyard the Admiralty controlled the election of its members of parliament, the aldermen and burgesses always voting for its nominees. Once elected, the members maintained their position largely by bribery and patronage, often in the form of placing contracts awarded by the Admiralty where they would be most likely to win or retain support for them. This state of affairs began when Admiral Sir Charles Wager was elected in 1714 and retained his seat for twenty years, during which period he was at one time or another Comptroller and Treasurer of the Navy and First Lord of the Admiralty. Seven other admirals also represented Portsmouth between 1721 and 1747, after which Sir Edward Hawke was chosen, probably in return for the trade he was bringing the town through his successes at sea, and continued to sit for it for the next twenty-one years, during part of which he was absent on service, though admittedly of the most distinguished kind. In addition, high-ranking naval officers and functionaries were often enrolled as burgesses and sometimes even as alderman.[6]

This servitude to the Admiralty was challenged in the second half of the century by two successive generations of the Carter family. The rise of this family had begun nearly a hundred years earlier when Roger Carter, a mason, married as his second wife Sarah Ridge, a member of one of the town's leading merchant families, and thus advanced his interests both socially and commercially. His son John (the same who brought the news of Queen Anne's death) continued the process by marrying the daughter of an alderman who was also a prominent Presbyterian and whose business partner he became. Though originally an Anglican, John adopted his wife's faith and was soon a generous supporter of the Presbyterian chapel. By the time he died in 1732 he had become a comparatively wealthy man.

It was, however, only with his son John Carter II, who became an alderman in 1744 and was elected mayor for the first of seven times in 1747, that the family began to take a lead in Portsmouth politics. A man of vast energy and determination who combined high principles with shrewdness and sometimes even unscrupulousness in an almost paradoxical fashion, he now embarked on a prolonged struggle with the Admiralty. It must be borne in mind that after the accession of the Whigs to power, both nationally and locally, on Anne's death in 1714, the party labels of Whig and Tory lost much of their significance. The triumph of the former was so complete that the rivalry of the two parties which had dominated the domestic politics of the previous thirty or forty years gave place to the struggles of divergent groups or factions within the ranks of the Whigs alone. Both centrally and locally these conflicts arose to a considerable but varying extent from personal reasons, usually combined in the localities with local issues. The struggle which now began in Portsmouth was a conflict of this kind; though perhaps Carter can be regarded, at any rate at first, as the leader of a young progressive group who resented the red tape and corruption of the Admiralty as well as its encroachment on the rights and privileges of the Corporation, and his opponents as ministerialists with a vested interest in supporting the governments of the day. Owing to the limitations of the sources, however, our knowledge of the details of events or sometimes of the reasons why they took place is incomplete.

The first battle, which Carter lost, began when he called a meeting at his house in Thomas Street, at which sixty-two new burgesses were elected, most of them members of the 'patriotic' or anti-ministerialist party. Eighteen of them were children, including Carter's two sons aged eight and five respectively. In the following year a lampoon was published in the shape of a satirical poem entitled *The Geese in Disgrace, Humbly inscribed to the Corporation of P—ts——h*, in which the Corporation (the 'Geese') were accused of subservience to the Admiralty in the nomination of M.P.'s, with special reference to Hawke's election four years earlier. But the ministerialists hit back with a threat to get the Navy contracts withdrawn, which would have ruined the town. This apparently nipped the movement against the Admiralty in the bud, at least for the time being, since another admiral, Sir William Rowley, was elected in 1754 as Hawke's colleague, which he remained until 1761.

There followed a long period during which the rivalry of the two groups must have smouldered without flaring up to a confrontation. Then about 1770 the conflict blazed up again, with the Carter party attacking the Corporation by bringing legal actions against its privileges and its charter. By 1772 they had come uppermost and Carter's eldest son John (who was knighted in the following year during a visit of George III to the town) became mayor. He was followed by his brother William, during whose mayoralty forty-three new burgesses were chosen from the friends and allies of the Carters, both resident and non-resident. Their opponents, however, replied by fastening upon the 1750 elections of minors to burgess-ship and bringing actions in their turn, as a result of which the young Sir John Carter, the rest of the former minors, and fifty-one others of their party were deprived of their status as burgesses. After that the rest of the struggle became an increasingly complicated and sometimes almost comic see-saw in which each group strove to oust the mayors, aldermen and burgesses of the other and replace them by its own partisans, employing lawsuits as weapons whenever possible. This occasionally resulted in stalemates during which the town was left almost without government. In 1775 there were only five aldermen; between that year and 1780 three mayors were ousted by *mandamus*, one of them being John Carter II himself in 1780; and after his successor's rapid resignation there was no mayor at all for four months. Eventually the death of the ministerialists' leader Alderman Linzee in 1782 ended this extraordinary struggle. Sir John Carter was again elected mayor and an entirely Carterite Corporation duly appointed thirty-seven new burgesses, twenty-eight of whom had previously been ousted. No aldermen of the other party were left, and the Carter influence remained paramount for half a century or more. The family controlled the parliamentary elections for the borough almost uninterruptedly until the Reform Act of 1832 and dominated municipal politics until long after the Municipal Corporations Act of 1835 had replaced the old machinery of town government by a more democratic system.

At the time of the 1782 victory the leaders of the Carter party were a homogeneous and primarily trading group, with strong interests in brewing. Sir John Carter, who had now taken the lead during his father's old age, had entered the distilling trade at the age of twenty-five and a few years later became manager of a brewery situated between High Street and Penny Street and belonging to his maternal grandfather William Pike, another prominent Dissenter. Several others of the group were also members of the congregation of High Street Chapel, which like many Presbyterian bodies elsewhere was at this time moving towards Unitarianism. Before 1828, when the repeal of the Test and Corporation Acts removed the statutory ban on the holding of public office by nonconformists, it was unusual but not unique for the government of a town to be in the hands of the Dissenting interest. This was made possible by two modifications of the law: the practice of 'occasional conformity', by which a Dissenter could qualify for office by taking the sacrament in a church at least once and obtaining a certificate that he had done so; and the ruling that anyone who had held office unchallenged for six months could not afterwards be challenged. In any case the challenge had to be made by way of a complaint to a justice of the peace, and in a town like Portsmouth (or Bristol, Norwich, Bridport or Bridgwater, which were in like case) it might be difficult to find one who would agree to receive it, even if he were not himself a nonconformist.

On public issues the Carter party supported what it presently becomes possible, with some caution, to resume calling the Whig interest. They naturally took part in the agitation for the repeal of the Test and Corporation Acts; they disliked the war against the American colonists, and were in favour of some measure of parliamentary reform. This last inclination produced the anomaly that since Portsmouth as a pocket borough was a typical example of the system the reformers wished to abolish, they were campaigning for its abolition even though it maintained them in power, perhaps because they were fairly confident that they could stay in control without it.[7]

8. The 'Great French Wars', 1793–1815

The quarter of a century in which the 'Second Hundred Years War' culminated—the Revolutionary (1793–1802) and Napoleonic (1803–15) Wars, the greatest in which the country had ever yet been engaged— intensified Portsmouth's activities as Britain's premier naval base and dockyard. Encampments of troops were frequently formed both on Southsea Common and near the barracks at Hilsea which had been built in 1780 and enlarged in 1794; the fortifications were strengthened further; and when invasion seemed likely volunteer corps, the Loyal and Independent Regiments of Volunteers, were raised in both Portsmouth and Portsea in 1797. The uniform of the Portsea Volunteers was

a round black hat with a band of bear fur over it; white feather with red top, black cockade, black stock, scarlet coat with gold wings and blue collar and the button-holes edged with gold, the skirts edged with white and finished with gold rosettes; white waistcoat, frilled shirt, blue pantaloons edged with scarlet cord, short black gaiters and shoes; hair frizzed and powdered, with a pigtail behind. The officers wore helmets.

Nevertheless the costume of the Portsmouth Volunteers was so much finer still that they were nicknamed 'the Golden Goldfinches'.[1]

A vivid but mainly unfavourable picture of Portsmouth in this time of war was painted in 1795 by one Dr George Princkard, whose outlook may have been somewhat biassed by the fact that he was waiting there for the departure of General Sir Ralph Abercrombie's expedition to the West Indies:

Portsmouth verifies to our experience all that we had heard of its un-pleasantness and vulgar immorality... The busy activity of the place occurs only at intervals, as when a fleet comes in or is about to sail, at which periods the town becomes all crowd and hurry for a few days, and then suddenly reverts to a languid intermission of dullness and inactivity.* The rent of houses and apartments, the price of provisions, etc., differ very much in times of peace and of war. Indeed, we are told that the

---

* Princkard had presumably not been near the dockyard.

houses and lodgings have their war price and their peace price, distinctly fixed ... In some quarters Portsmouth is not only filthy and crowded, but crowded with a class of low and abandoned beings who seem to have declared open war against every habit of common decency and decorum... The riotous, drunken and immoral scenes of this place perhaps exceed all others. .. Hordes of profligate females are seen reeling in drunkenness, or plying upon the streets in open day with a broad immodesty... To form to yourself an idea of these tender languishing nymphs, these lovely fighting ornaments of the fair sex, imagine a something of more than Amazonian stature, having a crimson countenance emblazoned with all the effrontery of Cyprian confidence and broad Bacchanalian folly; give to her bold countenance the warlike features of two wounded cheeks; a tumid nose, scarred and battered brows and a pair of blackened eyes with balls of red; then add... a pair of brawny arms fit to encounter a Colossus and... ankles like the fixed supporters of a gate... and thus you will have something very like the figure of a "Portsmouth Poll". Callous to every sense of shame, these daring objects reel about the streets, lie in wait at the corners, or... hover over every landing-place ... and each unhappy tar who has the misfortune to fall under their talons has no hope of escape till plucked of every feather... He is then left to sleep till he is sober, and awakes to return penniless to his ship, with much cause to think himself fortunate if an empty purse be the worst consequence of his long-wished-for ramble ashore.[2]

Princkard, however, expressed admiration for 'that new modern messenger, the telegraph, by which intelligence can be conveyed from this place to the Admiralty . . . in the short space of ten minutes'. By this he meant the system of giant wooden semaphores installed that year on hills* and other salient spots within sight of each other by telescope, the first being on Southsea Common near the present Clarence Pier and the last on the Admiralty roof, by which it presently proved possible to transmit a brief message even more quickly.[3] The original semaphore on Southsea Common was afterwards replaced by one on the Square Tower, and this in turn by another built on the Rigging Tower in the dockyard in 1833.

The anonymous visitor of 1807 already referred to† also left on record impressions which on the whole were not inconsistent with Princkard's strictures:

The town is low and aguish; the streets uncleanly and in many places wretched; but from the constant resort of seamen a busy scene is presented. You meet companies of three or four sailors, each with his trull under his arm, whom he has decked out in flaring ribbons and with

---

* The use of 'telegraph' for these semaphores led to several eminences being called 'Telegraph Hill', the nearest local example being that above South Harting near Petersfield.
† See above, p. 65.

whom he posts up and down the streets without any apparent object, from morning to night. At the crossing, if you are not upon your guard, you are in imminent peril of being run over by a midshipman driving a blind horse in a crazy jingling gig, as furiously as Jehu... Sometimes a low alehouse presents itself, with a *pas de deux* between Jack and a Portsmouth Parisot in the vestibule, to the elegant strains of two blind fiddlers. But the most entertaining scene of all is found in the coffee-houses, where every table is covered with fierce cocked hats and hangers and where every five minutes you hear—"Waiter! Get me a beef-steak; and bear a hand!"[4]

The same reporter also commented on the convicts, who since 1800 were being sent to Portsmouth in considerable numbers to help with the new works now in progress, and were housed in hulks in the harbour. Working in chains,

they were making a show of pulling a cable, but the progression of their labour was very imperceptible; and indeed it is matter of wonder how they can be brought to work at all, since I was informed ... that there are neither any indulgences for labour nor any punishments for indolence. Others of them came about the party begging, or selling small wares manufactured from bone. The guide warned us to take care of our pockets...[5]

The departure and on occasion the victorious return of fleets and squadrons were watched by cheering crowds, who were largest and most enthusiastic when Admiral Lord Howe landed after his victory of the Glorious First of June in 1794. But perhaps the supreme moment of this kind was Portsmouth's last glimpse of Nelson alive. Napoleon's shadow then lay dark and heavy over Europe. England alone still stood out against him, and when Nelson sailed to Trafalgar it was not known that the Emperor's great invasion scheme had already been abandoned. There were many admirals of distinction—even though 'Black Dick' Howe was now dead—but to the British people what stood between them and the dictatorship of 'Boney' was the genius of this frail little man who had already lost an arm and an eye in their service. When it was known that he had arrived at the George Hotel early one morning and was breakfasting before going aboard the *Victory*, huzzaing crowds gathered hastily in the High Street. To avoid them he left by the back door into Penny Street and a doorway through the walls and a bridge across the moat which can still be seen, instead of from the Sally Port* as usual. Before he could step into his boat, however, a racing

---

* There were two Sally Ports in Broad Street until 1847, the one referred to here (which still exists at the side of the Square Tower) being used by officers, and the other, higher up the street, by seamen and the general public. When Point Barracks were built in 1847 the latter disappeared. (GATES, *Records of the Corporation, 1835-1927*, p. 2).

delirious mob covered Southsea Common, crying 'God bless you, Nelson!' and pressing round him to shake his hand. His pale face glowing with emotion, the Admiral exclaimed 'I wish I had two hands, and then I could accommodate more of you!' Even when the boat had pushed off people ran waist-deep into the water to shout their gratitude to their hero. Tears trickled down the cheeks of some of the boat's crew at the sight, and Nelson, turning to Captain Hardy sitting beside him, said 'I had their huzzas before, now I have their hearts'.[6]

Similar, and yet very different, was the scene nine years later when again a great crowd gathered in the High Street to greet the man whose name is linked with Nelson's as the saviour of Europe from Napoleon. The allied sovereigns, believing their enemy to be safely caged at Elba, had come to Portsmouth to review the British Fleet. The ropemakers of the dockyard, in white jackets with purple sashes, had according to ancient custom headed the procession which conveyed the Prince Regent into the town. Blücher had waved to the crowd from the gallery of the Governor's House and declined requests for a lock of his hair on the ground that he had all too few already. But for the people the greatest moment was the arrival of the Duke of Wellington. Harnessing themselves to his carriage, they drew him in triumph through the streets. The Prince Regent clasped his hand and pompously proclaimed: 'England's glory is now complete! It wanted only the presence of Your Grace!' Nelson, who exulted and expanded in the sun of applause and flattery, would have been in the seventh heaven. The Iron Duke, who detested fuss and bombast, was probably intensely irritated.[7]

In Portsmouth politics the outbreak of war with revolutionary France in 1793 had produced a temporary reaction in favour of Toryism. To voice a wish or demand for change in public became difficult and dangerous. Already in 1792 the Corporation had been among those which voted addresses to the Crown in support of a proclamation against seditious writings that had just been issued, and later in the same year the town was also one of the many which formed associations 'for preserving Liberty and Property against Republicans and Levellers'. Nevertheless it is perhaps significant that the language of loyalty used by the Whiggish Corporation was rather more restrained than that of some other places. Instead of lauding 'our glorious constitution' and denouncing 'the nefarious endeavours of wicked, designing and ungrateful men' as Gosport, for instance, did, the ruling oligarchy of Portsmouth wrote more coolly that 'the government of this country by kings, lords and commons has by experience been happily proved to be the safeguard of our liberties'. The reactionary swing was never complete, however. Between 1790 and 1806 the town was represented in Parliament by the advanced liberal Thomas Erskine, the intimate friend of Charles James Fox and the defender of the Radicals Thomas Hardy, Thelwall and Horne Tooke when they were tried for treason in 1794. After their acquittal the *Hampshire Chronicle* (a Winchester paper founded in 1772 but representative of much Portsmouth opinion) proclaimed its sympathies by declaring that Erskine's 'glorious struggle on this occasion would make him for ever dear to mankind'. Not long before this the same paper had carried a series of articles on the corrupt representation of Hampshire by the county members and asserted that rotten and pocket boroughs were excrescences on the constitution.[8]

Underneath what thus survived in Portsmouth of reforming or advanced Whiggism there are traces of a deeper movement of working-class radicalism with roots in the dockyard and links with the mainly artisan London Corresponding Society. For some time there had been discontent in the yard, though it was economic rather than political in origin. In particular, when at the outbreak of the American War in 1775 the Admiralty in its anxiety to speed up production had introduced a piecework system the shipwrights resented this so much that they came out on strike, to which the Admiralty's answer was to dismiss them all and bring new men down from Deptford—though after the strike had collapsed the pressing needs of the war compelled the reinstatement of all but a few leaders. After the outbreak of the French Revolution and the Revolutionary War, however, there were stirrings of something more political. In 1795, when the Corresponding Society was striving to build up a national ultra-Radical organisation, there is some evidence of its activity in Portsmouth. It seems to have been giving special attention to the dockyard towns, and one of its leaders, John Binns, was despatched to Portsmouth but recalled when it was learnt that he was being shadowed and was liable to arrest; while in the following year the *Hampshire Chronicle* reported that 'sundry symptoms of democracy' (a word then virtually synonymous with revolution to all supporters of the established régime) had lately made their appearance in the town and in particular caps of liberty bearing the words 'Vive la République' had been affixed by night to the royal arms which ornamented the houses of two distributors of stamps and another substantial citizen who was druggist to the King's brother the Duke of Clarence.[9]

Besides this whisper of political extremism, the closing years of the century saw bread riots brought about by a run of bad harvests and by high taxation and the pressure of a swelling population not all of whom could be absorbed by the increased employment available in the dockyard; or if absorbed could not earn more than the low wages paid to labourers. It must be remembered in this connection that not only had the townward drift from the countryside begun but an appreciable number of seamen discharged from their ships did not make their way back home but preferred to stay on in Portsmouth, to which they had taken a liking—though not necessarily to the Navy. In April 1795, with prices rising:

several bodies of 4 or 500 persons assembled at different parts of. . . Portsea and put the inhabitants generally into the greatest fear. . . All the houses and shops were immediately shut, but those on which the mob were intent, viz., the butchers' and bakers', were either opened by their entreaty or broke open by them, when the meat of all descriptions was demanded at 4d. per pound and bread at 6d. per quarter. Those who complied with the demand were paid with exactness at the above price; but those who refused had their shops gutted, without receiving any more money than the mob chose to leave. The soldiers in the garrison, having in the morning demanded and obtained beef and mutton at 4d. per pound, could not be sent to quell a mob who only evinced a similar resolution. No other violence took place and... no personal injury happened to anyone.[10]

A year later, when after a temporary fall in the price of bread prices rose again, a large mob assembled in St George's Square, Portsea, consisting mostly of dockyard and Victualling Office workers. About a thousand of them came quietly into Portsmouth to state their grievance to Sir John Carter, who said that he would do what he could. The crowd then promised to disperse, but some did not do so and on their way back to Portsea destroyed the houses of several bakers. On the following night further demonstrations took place. Three of the leaders were arrested and put in the lock-up, which a crowd thereupon broke open and demolished. Troops had to be called out and more arrests made before the mob could be dispersed.[11]

A more positive and praiseworthy reaction produced by the food shortages and high prices was the formation by the dockyard workers of one of the earliest co-operative societies. In May 1796 some of them made an agreement to build a mill and bakehouse, subscribing over £800 for the purpose, 'for the cheaper supplying of bread and flour (and such other Necessaries of Life as they or the Majority shall think fit)'. The bread and/or flour was to be delivered to members' houses, both baker and customer having duplicate tickets to show the amount required. By 1802 the society had 880 members, and it maintained its existence throughout and beyond the war years.[12]

In 1800 the Mayor and magistrates announced that for the coming year no Assize of Bread would be set (that is, the customary price-fixing regulations would not be issued and no official attempts would be made to control food prices). Almost immediately they went up and there was further trouble. Two meetings were held on successive evenings, the second of which led to seven people being arrested, and the dockyard men distributed a handbill stating that they would buy no butter at more than ninepence a pound, no cream at more than the proportionate price, no milk at more than twopence a quart nor potatoes at more than sixpence a gallon. This was accompanied by a placatory statement that they regarded property as sacred, abhorred all proceedings which disturbed the public peace and would help to preserve it if required; after which they went on:

'To say that all of us are deprived of those things would be false; from our wages some of us procure them; but those with large families, as well as workmen out of the Dockyard, cannot procure a sufficiency of the necessaries of life'.

But if the (obviously skilled and more educated) dockyard workmen were taking a non-violent line there were others ready to threaten. Some doggerel lines surreptitiously posted up called on the rich to

'Repent before too late, the time is drawing nigh . . .
You grind us so our children can't get bread,
Consider this before you lose your head . . .
The halter's made,
The time is near at hand
That you must make
Your exit from this land'.

It was probably by the same hand that in order to give point to this threat three halters were hung up at the Lion Gate in Portsea with a paper underneath proclaiming

A caution
To the farmers, millers and bakers . . .
Each of you take your choice.
The greatest rogue
May have the greatest hoist'.[13]

But by far the most alarming event of these disturbed years was the great Spithead Mutiny of 1797.[14] This has usually been thought of, and even sometimes treated in writing, as if it had been a sudden and almost isolated outburst. But in fact, as Mr Alistair Geddes has shown,* 'disaffection amounting at times to mutiny was endemic in the Navy at Portsmouth, both before and after Spithead'. In 1780, 1781, on at least two occasions in 1783, in 1791, 1793, 1794, 1795, 1796 and again twice in 1798 mutinies or mutinous incidents occurred. The end of the American War in 1783, involving the long-awaited discharge of large numbers of men to whom arrears of pay were owing, naturally saw several such incidents. In March, even though the famous and popular Admiral Lord Howe had come down to Portsmouth and was stated to have 'quieted the minds' of some mutinous ships, the crews of the *Janus*, *Ganges* and *Proselyte* a few days later insisted on being instantly paid their wages and discharged from the Navy, otherwise they were determined 'to run their ships on shore and destroy them'. Letters were also sent to the Commander-in-Chief and to the Commissioner threatening to commit outrages upon them unless they exerted every means in their power to obtain the men's pay. Later in the year a body of seamen marched to London to present a petition to George III claiming that they had been pressed into the Service while their families at home experienced the most wretched state of indigence and despair

---

* In his admirable paper on 'Portsmouth during the Great French Wars' contributed to the *Portsmouth Papers* series.

and complaining of 'the wanton cruelty of many petty officers', especially in 'bestowing corporal punishment upon them when their occasional meeting with an old messmate induced them to trespass a little upon their allowance of time [in other words, to overstay their leave] and to become convivial in his company'. The petition also raised the perennial grievance of arrears of pay, but it received no satisfactory answer. About the same time the men of the *Raisonnable* refused to weigh anchor for Chatham, where they had been told they would be paid off, and demanded to be paid and discharged at Portsmouth. But when Admiral Montagu ordered the guns of the other ships and of Southsea Castle to be brought to bear on the *Raisonnable* and to sink her if necessary they returned to duty, which did not save three of their leaders from being court-martialled and hanged.

More trouble followed in the next decade. In 1791 a mutiny in Commodore Goodall's squadron on its arrival at Spithead was apparently prevented only by paying the men off immediately. In 1793 the crew of a frigate forwarded a complaint about pay to the Admiralty and when they got no answer barricaded themselves below and refused to sail, but the matter was dealt with by dispersing 75 of them to other ships; and in 1794 the crew of the *Culloden* mutinied and held control of their ship for several days. For this their leaders were afterwards hanged.[15]

The discontent of the lower deck had thus been boiling up for a considerable time before it boiled completely over in 1797. The seamen's pay had not been increased since the middle of the seventeenth century, on top of which it was liable to deductions that sometimes reduced it to half its nominal value. Moreover it was often anything up to two years or more in arrears, and was issued in full only when a ship was paid off and then in the form of tickets, which the men had to dispose of to sharks and bumboat-women at a heavy discount. Food was short and vile, and made shorter and worse by the ships' pursers appropriating the less unpalatable provisions in order to sell them privately. Discipline was maintained by formal and ferocious flogging supplemented all too often by less formal blows and beatings; and shore leave while in port was virtually unknown for fear of desertion, with the result that seamen might not see their wives and families (who were usually left dependent on poor relief) for years at a time. The high rate of desertion when opportunity offered was partly responsible for the lavish use of the press-gang* which, generally with brutal violence, not only snatched seamen from the privateers and the better-paid merchant service but (in time of war at least) sometimes swept up landsmen of the lower classes. There was indeed something of a vicious circle here. Men torn from their families or from the possibility of a more remunerative

---

* Though the proportion of voluntary enlistments in the Navy, except in the later stages of a war, was larger than is often thought. See M. LEWIS, *Social History of the Navy, 1793—1815*, pp. 90—5.

life at sea were naturally prone to desert; this in turn meant more work for the press-gang, and so the circle revolved.

As early as 1795 Captain Philip Patton, the transport officer at Portsmouth whose work it was to deal with the tenders bringing newly pressed men, reported to the First Lord of the Admiralty (who disregarded the warning) that a general mutiny was possible. In that year two acts of Parliament were passed for the recruitment of the Navy, the first of which required each county to raise a number of men roughly proportionate to its population, while the second called on each port to supply a quota of recruits. Local authorities met these requirements partly by a kind of gaol delivery, sending poachers, beggars, minor thieves and pickpockets, and partly by offering bounties for voluntary enlistment. The 'quota men' secured by this latter means tended to be better educated than the average seaman, as well as perhaps influenced by the democratic ideas that were beginning to circulate in the country; and some of them soon set to work to encourage and organise the almost dumb resentment that they found on the lower deck. The leading spirit of the Spithead mutiny, a 26-year-old quartermaster's mate named Valentine Joyce, was apparently of Portsmouth origin, since his father was an old soldier still serving in the garrison invalid corps and his parents had evidently lived in the town for at least a considerable time.

In 1797, after achieving a remarkable feat of undercover organisation, the men of the Channel Fleet sent a petition to Parliament about their pay and resolved to refuse to put to sea again after their current cruise ended unless their demands were heeded. On the evening of April 12 Captain Patton, more alert than most of his superiors, became aware of what was in the wind. Hastening ashore, he hurried to the newly installed 'telegraph' on Southsea beach and sent off the message 'Mutiny brewing at Spithead'. Relayed to a similar semaphore frame on Portsdown Hill, and thence to Telegraph Hill near Petersfield, Blackdown, Hanscomb, Cabbage Hill, Putney and Chelsea Hospital, it was read on the Admiralty roof in a very few minutes. My Lords sent Lord Bridport, the commander of the Fleet, instructions to prepare to put to sea and meanwhile order a squadron down to St Helen's, the usual starting-point for a cruise. When his subordinate Admiral Gardner duly tried to take a squadron down, he was met by an unanimous refusal to weigh anchor. Under Joyce's instructions each crew now elected two delegates to a committee which met aboard the flagship *Queen Charlotte* (Bridport being absent on shore). Lord Spencer, the First Lord of the Admiralty, then decided to go down to Portsmouth with two of his colleagues; but after their arrival they made no contact with the men and refused to discuss the other grievances of which they had drawn up a list, confining themselves to the pay issue, on which they were with difficulty persuaded by Bridport and others to meet the men's demands. When the choleric Gardner tried to force things on by a visit to the delegates in the flagship they confronted him angrily and ordered the guns to be mounted, the Fleet to be prepared for action and the officers who still remained on board placed in respectful confinement. At the same time they reiterated their demands, adding that even if they were conceded the King must proclaim a general pardon for them all before they would return to duty. Spencer, now alive to the seriousness of the situation, posted back to London and secured this. A hundred copies were immediately carried back to Portsmouth by an Admiralty rider using relays of horses, and Bridport read one to the delegates aboard the *Queen Charlotte* and made a speech promising redress of all grievances which was received with cheers. The mutiny seemed to be over.

Among the civilian population of Portsmouth there was much sympathy with the men's demands. They were growing tired of the war, which had brought to the town many wives and children of seamen who, being ill-paid or unpaid and not allowed to leave their ships, could neither care for them nor send them home, so that they became dependent on poor relief and swelled the poor rates which Portsmouth householders had to pay. For several years the Mayor and aldermen had petitioned the Government for relief, but without result. To many townsfolk, indeed, the difference between a fleet controlled by the Admiralty and one controlled by the delegates may have been that the latter, by allowing the men to come ashore to parade and make crude speeches, were giving publicans and shopkeepers a chance to do a little more trade than usual. And naturally the many local relatives of seamen in the Fleet, like Joyce's parents, must almost certainly have sympathised with them. Where the *Hampshire Chronicle's* sympathies lay was made evident by its printing the men's demands in full and emphasising the orderliness of their behaviour.

But now came what was really the second Spithead Mutiny. Parliament was slow in passing the legislation needed to implement the increase in pay which had been granted, and the Admiralty not only still refused to meet the men's demands in full but sent down orders to the captains of ships to make preparations (most of which were all too obvious) to suppress mutiny by force. This provoked a fresh outburst and in a collision aboard the *London* between officers and men three of the latter were mortally wounded. The angry delegates demanded that they should be ceremonially buried in Kingston churchyard and that a funeral procession of seamen should be allowed to march through Portsmouth to escort them thither. This demand was furiously rejected by the military authorities, who had prepared the garrison to withstand attack, manned the fortifications, raised the drawbridges, trained the guns of the shore batteries on the Fleet, and were not minded to admit the enemy—as they considered them—within the walls. But at the very moment when an armed clash and further bloodshed seemed probable Sir John Carter, who was mayor again at the time, intervened and arranged a compromise. The coffins of the dead seamen were landed at the Common Hard at Portsea, where they were met by contingents from the ships who had disembarked at a different point and had been led through Portsmouth by Sir John himself and another magistrate. At the Hard the procession took up the coffins and made its way by a less provocative route to Kingston, still accompanied by the two magistrates. Not only were the Mayor's injunctions to keep the peace scrupulously obeyed by the seamen, but they even went so far as to lock up two of their number who had taken too much to drink and were showing signs of becoming quarrelsome. For his intercession Carter was violently abused in authoritarian and reactionary circles, and of course by his now discomfited local political opponents. An anonymous letter denouncing him as a revolutionary and a traitor was sent to the Home Secretary, who sent it on to him with an assurance that he had the confidence of the Government* and an offer to issue a reward for the discovery of the writer. Sir John, however, declined the proposal.

Meanwhile the alarmed Government had not only rushed through Parliament a bill approving the addition to the naval estimates of the sum necessary to cover the increases in pay which the seamen demanded, but hit on the brilliant though belated idea of sending down Admiral Lord Howe as a special emissary and plenipotentiary to deal with their remaining complaints. 'Black Dick' Howe, whose saturnine and normally uncompromising face could break into a surprisingly sunny smile, was both the leading and the most popular British admiral of the generation before Nelson. Although he was 71 years of age, retired and gouty, he instantly set off for Portsmouth throughout a wild and stormy night, accompanied by Lady Howe. On arrival he left her at the Governor's house, set out by barge for the flagship, which was now lying off St Helen's, rejected all offers to help him up the side, had the ship's company called to the quarter-deck, and started in to talk to them as a man to men, with no reproaches, no standing on his dignity and no refusal to recognise the authority of the delegates. For three days he went from ship to ship, talking, listening and making speeches. On the fourth he met the assembled delegates and agreed to recommend to the Admiralty (by the 'telegraph') the supersession of 59 unpopular officers and the concession of all the men's demands except shore leave, which they had not pressed to an issue.

On the next day Howe was escorted ashore by a procession of boats and received at Point by 'an immense multitude' cheering itself hoarse and by his delighted wife. They walked together to the Governor's house, where Joyce stepped forward to arrange for a more formal ceremony on the morrow and was invited in by Howe to drink a glass of wine with him. At dawn next morning the procession of boats reappeared and the delegates landed at the Sally Port, from which they marched to the Governor's house, headed by a band playing 'God Save the King' and 'Rule Britannia' alternately. After Howe had invited them

---

* The Home Secretary, the Duke of Portland, was a former Whig.

all in to drink wine with him and then taken them on to the balcony to receive the thunderous applause of the crowd, he and Lady Howe walked back with them to the Sally Port with the bands—for the Marine band and various ships' bands had now arrived—blaring away in front. Here it seemed as if every boat in the Solent was waiting to take part in the triumphal procession. Howe went first to the flagship and then to every ship in the Fleet, reading the royal pardon on the quarter-deck of each and showing it afterwards to the few seamen who could read. At six o'clock the boats returned once more to the Sally Port, with the old warrior so exhausted that he had to be lifted from his barge. The seamen who did so carried him on their shoulders back to the Governor's house with the Union Jack held above his head, through crowds such as the town had never seen before, yelling their lungs out. Probably no monarch nor any other national hero, not even Nelson—though had he returned alive from Trafalgar this scene might have been matched—ever had such a reception in Portsmouth. It was the last of the long line of victories Black Dick had won for England—the last and perhaps the greatest too. He must have slept well that night, so shortly before he fell asleep for ever.

Or perhaps it would only have been the greatest of his victories if it had been a complete and final one. For the example of the Spithead Mutiny sparked off another at the Nore in which 'there is some evidence of direct instigation'* by French Jacobin revolutionaries and which was more threatening and longer maintained; though after three weeks it collapsed and was visited with summary punishment. Even at Portsmouth there were later sputters of unrest. In June and July 1797 four of the crew of the *Poupée* and one man from the *Phoenix* were sentenced to be hanged for mutiny and several others suffered lesser penalties; while in 1798 one man from the *Adamant* was hanged and another flogged round the Fleet, and some members of the *Pluto*'s crew were said to have threatened to take the ship to the French. Nor must the gains of the Spithead mutiny be exaggerated. It improved the seamen's pay and rations somewhat, but perhaps the best that can be said is that it did something to open the public's eyes to the conditions of lower deck life and from then on, though only little by little, the seamen began to receive better treatment.

---

* PROFESSOR E. P. THOMPSON, *The Making of the English Working Class*, p. 167.

9. 'Peace, retrenchment and reform', 1815–35

At the beginning of the nineteenth century the urban pattern of Portsea Island showed three distinct settlements—Portsmouth, Portsea and now Landport, with the nucleus of a fourth, Southsea, beginning to take shape in the next two decades. Towards the end of the century the Rev. Robert Dolling, writing retrospectively in 1896 of his *Ten Years in a Portsmouth Slum*, could say that Portsmouth was

composed of four separate towns. When Portsmouth [itself] and Portsea, the former thronged with soldiers, the latter with sailors—High Street, Portsmouth, being a kind of parade-ground [and] the Hard, Portsea, a kind of inland quarter-deck—burst their bonds and the moats were removed they developed on the one hand into Southsea, inhabited mostly by half-pay officers, with many hotels and lodging-houses, and in the other direction into Landport and Kingston, inhabited mostly by artisans in the dockyard.

According to a local guide-book of the same year, whereas to the Navy Chatham and Rochester were 'the two towns' and Plymouth, Devonport and Stonehouse 'the three towns', Portsmouth, Portsea, Landport and Southsea were known as 'the four towns'. Even to-day, a hundred years after the demolition of the constricting fortifications which were so much responsible for the separateness of these four areas, it is barely ceasing to be clear-cut.

The growth in the size and activities of the dockyard during the Revolutionary and Napoleonic Wars, together with the increased numbers of the armed forces stationed in the area, had naturally meant a marked rise in the population of all but the first of the four. Between the censuses of 1801 and 1811 the figures for the borough of Portsmouth, which included all four of them, rose from 33,226 to 41,587; but within this rise there was a drop of 9.4%, from 7,839 to 7,103, in the old walled town. This has been ascribed chiefly to the absorption into the Services of many former civilian inhabitants who by the latter date (if still alive) were serving elsewhere.[1]

During the wars the dockyard had employed more than 4,000 men, or 36% of the estimated labour force of the borough. But with peace came redundancies and a reduction in the number of men for whom there was work in the yard. This was not due to any curtailment of shipbuilding there, for there was actually an increase in that, but to a severe cut-back in repairs and refits. In the war years these had been much more important than new construction, thanks to the Admiralty's policy of making the royal dockyards responsible for them, while on the whole turning for shipbuilding to merchant and private yards like Buckler's Hard near Beaulieu or Bursledon on the Hamble or those of the Thames.[2] But in March 1816 300 mechanics were dismissed with one week's pay and over 50 labourers had to leave with them. Two months later 90 of the oldest mechanics in the yard, some of them with fifty years' service to their credit, were superannuated on bounties of from £14 to £24 per annum. After that the Admiralty decided to cut the wages of those still employed instead of ordering more discharges, since there was no means of alternative employment. In 1817 the pay of the remaining dockyard men was reduced to the previous lowest peace limit; in spite of which there was a further reduction in 1821. Later in that same year orders were issued for the men to work only five days a week instead of six, which meant an overall loss of £600 a week to the 3,000 men still employed; and eighty more were superannuated.[3]

At that time a large number of convicts were also being used on work in the yard, as well as in other Government establishments; and a memorial prepared at a town meeting for presentation to the Admiralty asked for this to be discontinued in order that honest men should not be deprived of their livelihood. This request was not granted, but the discharges ceased about six weeks later, presumably because of the memorial. The dockyard officials also, as a palliative, tried giving mechanics inferior work to do until times should improve. In 1825 a return was made to working six days a week; but the decline of the yard reached its nadir in 1830, when the establishment was cut down to 2,000, wages were once more reduced considerably and the practice of paying workmen 'chip-money' amounting to about two shillings a week (initiated in 1801 in lieu of their former and much abused privilege of carrying chips of timber out of the yard) was discontinued in order to avoid the discharge of about one-sixth of the men still at work.[4]

The repercussions on the town of this decline were greeted with a positive howl of exultation and with even more than his usual exaggeration by that robust hater of towns in general, William Cobbett, in his *Rural Rides*. In 1821, on the strength of what he had been told at an inn in Chatham by a gentleman who was probably a Chathamite with a dislike of Portsmouth and a personal grievance into the bargain, he wrote almost gloatingly of

the house-distress in that enormous wen which during the war was stuck on to Portsmouth. Not less than fifty thousand people had been drawn together there! These are now dispersing. . . Whole streets are deserted, and the eyes of the houses knocked out by the boys that remain. The

jackdaws. . . are beginning to take possession of the Methodist chapels.*
The gentleman told me that he had been down to Portsea to sell half a
street of houses left him by a relation, and that nobody would give him
anything for them further than as very cheap fuel and rubbish.[5]

The figures, however, hardly bear Cobbett out. What they do show is
a marked slowing-down in the rate of the borough's population growth
in the twenty-five years after the war; from 25.2% between 1801 and
1811 to 12.4% in the next decade (41,587 to 46,743, most of this rise
probably occurring in the first four years while the country was still at
war), 7.8% (to 50,389) between 1821 and 1831, and 5.2% (to 53,032)
between 1831 and 1841. After that the population leapt upwards again
by 36.2% and 31.9% respectively in the following two decades.[6] But the
previous deceleration was far from being the 'absolute tumbling down'
that Cobbett had also called it.[7]

Nevertheless the only considerable enterprise attempted in the post-
war decades ended in failure. This was a plan, or rather a series of
plans, for inland water communication by river and canal between
London and Portsmouth, which had originated in the later war years
but was only now attempted to be carried into effect. The navigational
hazards of the sea-passage between the Isle of Wight and the Thames in
the sailing-ship era had been complicated further during the Napoleonic
War by the very considerable risk from French privateers who darted
out of their Channel ports to strike at passing merchantmen and made
off again with their prizes within perhaps only a single night and day. To
avoid these dangers, natural and man-made, was the purpose of these
plans.

From 1802 onwards, therefore, some of the leading civil engineers of
the day put forward rival schemes for water communication between
London and Portsmouth, and one, William Jessop, even proposed an
ambitious project for a horse-operated railway. At first nothing came of
any of these plans because of the powerful opposition of landowners who
did not want their estates and privacy disturbed; but progress began to
be made when attention was turned to the idea of joining together the
existing 'navigations' (i.e., deepened, straightened and therefore
navigable rivers) of the Wey (a tributary of the Thames) and the Arun,
since if this could be done it would only remain to link the Arun to
Portsmouth and through water communication would at last be
established. In 1813–16 a Wey and Arun Junction Canal was built, and
the Duke of Norfolk, the Earl of Egremont (who owned Petworth
House) and several enterprising Portsmuthians who hoped among
other things to win freights away from the coasting vessels which traded
with the Camber forthwith proposed a Portsmouth and Arundel Canal

---

* Actually Methodism seems to have maintained reasonably
continuous progress.

to complete the inland water passage from the capital. An authorizing act was passed in 1817 and the work began at Ford on the Arun below Arundel in the next year. In 1822 the Portsmouth section, ending in a basin where Arundel Street now meets Commercial Road, was opened amid much rejoicing; and by the next year the canal was completed throughout. By 1831, however, it became evident that the traffic which it had been hoped to wrest from the coasters was not forthcoming, and such through trade as had been created between London and Portsmouth soon died away in face of the difficulties of the route, which involved six different canals or navigations with consequent transhipments and tolls. After 1840, when the railways began to appear, the through trade ceased altogether, and soon after the middle of the century the canal went out of business except for a 4½-mile cut from Chichester Harbour to Chichester. This struggled on for another fifty years until it too became disused about 1906. From first to last the company had never paid a dividend.

The continued, though slow, increase in the overall population of the borough in the twenty-five or so years after the war was of course mainly due to the growth of the suburbs of Landport, Kingston and now Southsea; though Portsea, which should by this time be counted as a twin town rather than a suburb, also showed some expansion. In the old town, though its figures rose slightly, a breakdown separating civilians from Service personnel suggests that the numbers of the former went on dropping until the 1840s, a phenomenon which has been attributed to the movement of people away to the suburbs from the cramped conditions of a walled town, made progressively worse by the continued expansion of the military establishments that were responsible for this slight overall rise.[10] In the 1820s the Colewort Barracks, the oldest in Portsmouth,* were much enlarged and the Clarence Barracks in St Nicholas Street, named in honour of George IV's brother the Duke of Clarence who succeeded him as William IV, and the large Cambridge Barracks between the upper ends of High Street and Penny Street were built. A military hospital was also established in 1833–4 a little north of the Lion Gate which was one of the two entrances to Portsea through its fortifications, the other being the Unicorn Gate.[11]†

The most strking urban development was undoubtedly that of Southsea. As Dr R. C. Riley has emphasised in his monograph on its growth,[12] it was unlike many other south-coast resorts in that it did not originally owe its rise to Victorian prosperity and the habit of holidaying by the seaside, but grew up rather as a residential suburb in which officers of both Services and dockyard officials and workmen lived or to which they retired. Only later did a considerable number of the monied

---

* See above, p57..
† The Lion and the Unicorn Gates were so called from the figures on their respective entablatures.

middle classes and summer visitors join them, creating an atmosphere which continued to attract many who were not compelled to live in the great industrial areas. It was almost entirely a nineteenth-century creation, for till 1800 the whole area that was to become Southsea consisted of marshes (the Great and Little Morasses shown on early maps), fields and gardens. There were only two buildings on Southsea Common, both taverns; the Five Cricketers, which was a haunt of smugglers in the seventeenth and eighteenth centuries, and the Wheelbarrow Cottage.[13]*

The Common itself was originally the waste of the manor of Froddington granted by William the Conqueror to William of Warenne, and was at first known as Froddington Heath. During the Middle Ages armies had several times been assembled there, and large camps of troops had also been formed on it during the Seven Years War and the Revolutionary War with France. It had come to be called Southsea Common after the building of Southsea Castle by Henry VIII. Later it reverted to the Crown and was granted to the Leeke family, who sold it to the Government in 1785 when additional land near the Castle was needed for military purposes. This military value of the Common prevented Victorian speculators from building along the line of the shore and so has created a substantial strip of land free from buildings between the sea and the built-up part of Southsea; but the nature of the Common itself would in any case have precluded early development, since large parts of it consisted of these ill-drained marshlands, interspersed with scrub and gorse-bushes. Thus in the early nineteenth century Southsea grew to the north of the Common, away from the sea, largely on land owned by Thomas Croxton, who 'must rank as its first successful speculator', but about whom little is known.

Croxton Town, comprising only a few streets by 1810, formed the core of early Southsea. As yet most of its houses were inhabited by artisans, but a middle-class element soon developed when the first of many terraces fronted by ornamental gardens began to appear, and by 1830 Southsea had grown out of this artisan Croxton Town into a 'middle-class outlier of the dockyard and garrison'. From their detached villas set among trees in their own grounds most of the local 'nobility and gentry' who now lived there had an uninterrupted view of the sea or could watch troops drilling and manoeuvring on the Common or the officers of the garrison and members of other clubs 'exercising at the athletic game of cricket', to quote a contemporary guide-book. In the winter there was snipe-shooting to the east of Southsea Castle; and in the summer bathing flourished on the beach as it never had in the previous century when it was confined within the harbour, where the small area of sand had limited the number of bathing-machines. Here

---

* The Cricketers has disappeared, but there is still a Wheelbarrow public-house on the original site.

on the beach the protection given by the Isle of Wight kept the waves moderate and its slope meant that the machines were never more than a few yards from deep water, thus avoiding 'the long and unpleasant exposure which is experienced at other places'. A modest wooden pump-room with baths and a reading-room was built on the site of the present Clarence Pier and developed a few years later by a new pro-prietor, Henry Hollingsworth, into a more elaborate combination of baths and assembly rooms. From the Duke of Clarence, who visited the establishment in 1824, Hollingsworth got leave to call it the Royal Clarence Promenade Rooms; and when the Duke came to the throne in 1830 the title was changed to the King's Rooms.

But though Hollingsworth's enterprise had done something to give Regency Southsea a reputation as a minor watering-place it was hardly yet a resort in the sense of being dependent on visitors. There was not much accommodation for them outside the terraces; merely a couple of taverns and one rather more pretentious hotel, the Bush, which was nevertheless more of a place where travellers could put up for a night or two than a base from which the waters could be taken; for the King's Rooms were non-residential and patronised less by visitors than by naval and military officers and the local gentry.

It was during twenty-one of these post-war years that John Pounds was carrying on the work of teaching his 'little wagabonds'. Besides reading and writing he also taught many of the boys to cook their own plain food and mend their own shoes, sent them to a Sunday school, and in order to enable them to make a creditable appearance there begged clothing from his friends which they were allowed to put on at his house on Sunday mornings and return to him in the evenings after he had taken them to chapel. So far as he could he acted as doctor and nurse for his pupils' ailments, and made bats, balls, crossbows and shuttlecocks for their games. Once a week in summer he took them for a day's excursion out of the foetid streets and courts in which they lived, limping along with them between the fields and up into the good clean air on top of Portsdown Hill, where they picnicked, played, and feasted their eyes on the panorama stretching from the downs of the Isle of Wight and the men-of-war lying at Spithead to the spire of Chichester Cathedral far away. To get books for them he turned to Dr. Russell Scott, the minister of High Street Unitarian Chapel, a powerful preacher known as 'the Oracle of the South', and afterwards to his successor the Rev. Henry Hawkes. After his death in 1839 his work came to the knowledge of Dr Thomas Guthrie of Edinburgh, who was greatly encouraged and influenced by it in the establishment, with other philanthropists, of the Ragged School movement. In consequence Pounds is now generally regarded as one of the chief inspirers of this movement, though not (as is sometimes stated) its founder.[14]

The government of Portsmouth remained firmly in the hands of the Carter party for a generation and more. It was completely in the control

14 John Dickens, father of Charles Dickens
Portsmouth City Museums

15 Birthplace of Charles Dickens   *Portsmouth City Museums*

16 The George Inn, c. 1805 *Drawn by M. Snafe*

17 Anchor Lane in Portsmouth Dockyard in the nineteenth century *Portsmouth City Museums*

18 The Grand Naval Review; yachts taking out passengers to view the Fleet, sketched from Southsea Common *Portsmouth City Museums*

19 Southsea between 1861 and 1866; water colour by Pernet *Portsmouth City Museums*

20 Bird's-eye view of Portsmouth Harbour
Panorama by permission of Councillor F. A. J. Emery-Wallis

21 Southsea Beach, showing memorials near
to Clarence Pier *Portsmouth City Museums*

22 Brunel's block-making machinery
Science Museum, London

23 Brunel's block-making machinery
Portsmouth City Museums

24 Enterprise House *Portsmouth City Engineers*

of the mayor and aldermen, who alone could give orders for the disposal of the corporate funds, the sale of Corporation property, the leasing of the Corporation lands and so forth, and also had the power of making bye-laws, though they seldom exercised it. On the eve of the reform of the municipal corporations in 1835 four of the ten aldermen* (who were elected for life by the mayor and their fellow aldermen out of the burgesses and need not be resident) were Carters, two more were nearly related to them and another was distantly related. Five out of these seven were non-resident and all ten had been appointed for party and in most cases family reasons. The election of the mayor had become a matter of form—there was only one contest, in 1812, in the last sixty years of the old Corporation's life—but since he had to reside within the borough it was among the five resident aldermen that the mayoralty rotated. The burgesses, chosen by the mayor and aldermen, had few privileges, but since these included a vote for the members of parliament for the borough they were always selected for party reasons and care was taken to keep their numbers small and manageable. Advantage was also taken of the fact that like the aldermen they need not be resident, to choose Carter relatives or supporters living at a distance. On the eve of the Reform Act of 1832 which threw the parliamentary franchise in boroughs open to all holders of houses with a rental value of £10 a year and upwards there were in Portsmouth only 46 burgesses, mostly non-resident;† but another 46, all resident,‡ were at once elected, since the act provided that burgesses who lived within seven miles of the borough were to keep their votes. Whether burgesses had the right of inspecting the Corporation accounts and other books was doubtful; they had never done so nor had any of them ever asked to do so, though members of the ruling body assured the commissioners of enquiry who visited Portsmouth prior to the Municipal Reform Act of 1835 that they would be allowed to see them if they wished, whether a right existed or not. Such trading privileges as they had once possessed had long since lapsed; and apart from the occasional exercise of the parliamentary franchise the only regular business in which they took part—and that a nominal one—was the election of the mayor and magistrates.[15]

'It can hardly be necessary', reported the visiting commissioners in 1833, 'to point out the complete closeness of this system; for a long series of years it has been exercised with the undisguised purpose of confining the whole municipal and political power to a particular party [the Whigs], and almost to a particular family'.[16] But although there

---

* Although the charter of 1627 stipulated for twelve aldermen this number was by no means always reached.

† Only eight lived within the borough and two more within seven miles of it.

‡ One lived in Gosport, but since his business was in Portsmouth he was counted a resident.

was monopoly of power and shameless nepotism (which after all was typical of the time) in appointments to municipal office, there was no corruption such as existed at Leicester, where Corporation funds were misused, the town charities perverted into bribes to win support, Corporation lands sold or leased cheaply to members and adherents of the ruling faction and the grant of public-house licences made sub-servient to party purposes.[17] It is true that when at the end of the Napoleonic War the Portsmouth magistrates (the Mayor, late Mayor and three senior aldermen), having concluded that since there were more than 230 licensed houses in the borough their number ought to be reduced, decreed that in future no licence would be granted for any house for which an excise licence had not been taken out in the previous year, there were some who thought and said that this rule had been laid down for the benefit of Pike's Brewery*, in which several of the Carters and their relatives were partners or otherwise largely interested. This charge seems to have been quite unfounded, however; nor could the investigating commissioners discover any instance of preferential treatment given to members of the Carter party in the granting of licences. All sales of Corporation land seem to have been made with perfect fairness and for its full value; and the commissioners 'did not find . . . any want of confidence in the magistrates or complaint of the manner in which they had performed their duties'; though they were inclined to think that they were too few in number considering the size of the population.[18] In short, Portsmouth was a close borough but not a corrupt one; the Carter party were determined to keep control of it by the methods common to the day, but otherwise they were decent enough people, by and large; or as the commissioners put it: 'That no instances can be traced of municipal corruption seems attributable, not to any correcting principle in the system, but merely to the absence of evil intentions in those who have been accidentally placed at its head'.[19]

With one short interval, the parliamentary representation of the borough was also controlled by the Carter party during this period, in the Whig interest. For virtually the whole of it one of the two seats was held by Sir John Carter's only son John, from his victory at a bye-election in 1816 until his death at the early age of 49 in 1838. In 1827 he took the surname of Bonham-Carter after inheriting the bulk of the estates and wealth of his relative Thomas Bonham of Petersfield. The interval in the completeness of the Carters' control referred to above occurred when in 1818 John's fellow-member Admiral Markham, a Whig whom Sir John Carter had started on his political career, was ousted by a Tory brother-admiral, Sir George Cockburn, who seems to have temporarily outbribed him. Since Cockburn was a lord of the Admiralty against which the Carters had battled in the previous century, this was a defeat for the family, though only a brief one, for in 1820

---

* See above, p. 78.

Markham turned the tables on his rival. From 1826 John Bonham-Carter was partnered by Francis Thornhil Baring, grandson of the founder of the famous financial house of Baring Brothers and Company, who later rose to eminence as Chancellor of the Exchequer and then First Lord of the Admiralty, and after representing Portsmouth for thirty-nine years was raised to the peerage as Lord Northbrook. Both were strong supporters of the Whigs' Reform Bill which after a titanic struggle was passed in 1832; although this placed Bonham-Carter and his family and local supporters (hundreds of whom celebrated the victory by an open-air dinner in St George's Square) in the peculiar position of fighting to destroy the system which gave them political control of the borough. He himself once put this position pithily by saying: 'We keep the borough of Portsmouth *close* for the purpose of making sure of two members to vote for throwing *open* all the boroughs in the kingdom'.[20] But though there was in Portsmouth a strong element of dissatisfaction with the closeness and exclusiveness of the Corporation and a good deal of jealousy of the Carters' control,[21] the fact that Bonham-Carter and Baring, after being elected thrice under the close system, were re-elected thrice more under the open one suggests that the politics of the party, at least, matched those of the majority of the townsfolk. Nor was the Carters' position changed very much when the Municipal Corporations Act of 1835 put an end to the closeness of the Corporation of Portsmouth as the Act of 1832 had put an end to it as a close parliamentary borough. John Bonham-Carter's cousin Edward Carter, who managed what was virtually the family brewery and had been mayor when John was first elected to Parliament in 1816, was again elected twenty years later as the first mayor of the new dispensation; and the family continued to exert influence on the town's affairs until late in the century.[22]

10. Expansion resumed, 1835–60.

The borough of Portsmouth had previously included only Portsmouth town itself, the satellite town of Portsea and part but not all of the rest of Portsea parish, while the remainder of the island, known as the Gildable, remained under the jurisdiction of the county magistrates. By the Reform Act of 1832, however, it had been enlarged for parliamentary purposes to include the whole of the parish of Portsea; that is, all the island except the Hilsea enclave.[1] The Municipal Corporation Act of 1835 extended its municipal limits correspondingly, divided it into six wards,* and placed it under the government of a town council consisting, besides the mayor elected annually by its members, of forty-two councillors elected by the ratepaying householders for the term of three years and fourteen aldermen elected by the councillors for six years, one half retiring every three. Former burgesses who did not qualify as ratepayers retained municipal franchise, but their number naturally gradually diminished.[2] Council meetings were to be held in public and accounts had to be audited annually by elected auditors. The property of the old corporations was transferred to the new bodies, but they did not as yet receive any great extension of authority. If they wished, they might take over the powers previously exercised by improvement commissioners where, as in Portsmouth, these existed, but they were not obliged to do so and many councils, of which Portsmouth's was one, limited themselves to assuming the commissioners' former control of the watch or police, leaving them to continue in existence for other business. The new councils were also authorised to levy rates, whether they had done so before or not.

On the other hand the benches of magistrates were now separated from the town councils; the magistrates, though they ceased to be appointed according to the local constitution of each individual town (and normally, as in Portsmouth, to be automatically the mayor and senior members of the Council), were not to be elected by the house-holders—to the Radicals' great disappointment—on the ground that

---

* In 1881 it was redivided into fourteen wards, since the original six had become very unequal in population.

impartial justice was incompatible with party electioneering. In form they became nominees of the Crown through the Home Office, though in practice a politically sympathetic government (as the Whig ministry naturally was towards Portsmouth) would pay much attention to the recommendations of a town council in making these appointments. The power of licensing public houses, which in the past had been open to abuse for political advantage, remained with the magistrates and was not entrusted to the councils. Nor was provision made for the connection that grew up afterwards between the corporations and the government departments at Whitehall, whereby the latter both aided and controlled the former by grants in aid of local rates. These developments and the gradual accretion to the new corporations of one power after another were nevertheless made possible by the Act of 1835.

Most of the new corporations immediately seized the opportunity to set up more modern police forces on the model of the Metropolitan Police established a few years previously, taking over (as aforesaid) the Improvement Commissioners' watch powers where necessary and setting up their own watch committees. At the time of the extinction of the old Corporation there had been thirteen constables for the borough and eleven for Buckland and Kingston, where several recent cases of body-snatching had caused a watch-house to be built in St Mary's churchyard. There were also a number of watchmen in Portsea, though none in old Portsmouth at the time; and Landport had a private night-watch of six men paid by subscription among the inhabitants. Private watches of this kind had also been raised from time to time in other parts of the borough. The new force of thirty men, one-third of whom came from the previous constabulary, included former victuallers, shop-keepers, butchers, wheelwrights, seamen, labourers, a carver and gilder and a hairdresser. At first they had no uniform, but after a few months it was decided to issue them with blue frock-coats and trousers, top-hats, greatcoats, capes and belts. Perhaps partly because of the force's miscellaneous origin, its first years were marred by bad feeling among the men, arising from the disparity in the pay of the various grades, and in 1839 it was reorganised to consist of a superintendent, three inspectors, three sub-inspectors and twenty-four constables. Applicants had to be under forty and at least 5'7" tall. Only thirteen of the former officers were retained in the new force, of which Captain Robert Elliott, late of the 82nd. Regiment, a ranker who had won his commission in the field for gallantry at the storming of Badajoz during the Peninsular War, was appointed the first superintendent. Watch-houses or (to use the later term) police-stations were established in the Town Hall, St George's Square in Portsea, and in Landport.[3]

Another of the new Corporation's first acts was to pull down the old Town Hall of 1739, which stood like its predecessor in the middle of the High Street, crushing part of it into two narrow thoroughfares. With the aid of a public subscription it was now replaced by a new Guildhall, along with a market house and the police station, on the south side of the street near the corner of Pembroke Street. The Guildhall, however, was presently let for the use of the County Court, and till 1862 the Corporation met in the sessions room and council chamber over the borough gaol. This had been built in 1805–9, fronting Penny Street and stretching back to St Nicholas Street, and had replaced an older smaller and inconvenient prison. Though enlarged about 1838 and having room for about eighty prisoners, the new gaol was so badly constructed that it had no facilities for classifying them and segregating the young from the old and the first offenders from the hardened criminals.[4]

The population of the borough, after twenty-five years of relative stagnation or at best slow progress, began to rise again rapidly in the 1840s, during which it grew by almost 20,000 from 53,032 to 72,096 in 1851, a growth rate which exceeded that during the Napoleonic War.[5] In the 1850s it rose by a further 23,000 to over 95,000. The main reason for this renewed expansion seems to have been a fresh increase in employment in the dockyard, whose labour force swelled again to 6,000 in the 'forties. This was due partly to the 'naval revolution' which was then taking place and whose main features were the change from sail to steam propulsion and from wooden walls to iron hulls, and secondly to a series of scares of invasion by the French.* The Crimean War which interrupted and temporarily calmed these by bringing Britain and France into alliance against Russia also served as a further stimulus to dockyard activity. Between 1843 and 1855 seventeen acres were added to the yard on the north and east in order to accommodate a large steam-basin and four new docks. This had the effect of cutting Portsea off from the harbour on its northern side, though the Admiralty afterwards gave its inhabitants access to it by the construction of the Anchor Gate which led on to the Hard. This gate, however, had to be sacrificed to further dockyard extension in 1897.[6]

During the 1820s and 1830s not many investment projects had been promoted locally, but in this more favourable period that followed a number of enterprises were floated from 1838 onwards, chiefly in transport. These included the Floating Bridge Company (1838), the Camber Docks improvement undertaken by the Corporation in 1839, the opening of the first horse-omnibus service in 1840 and the formation of the Portsmouth Harbour Pier Company in 1846. In addition to these locally-sponsored projects the London, Brighton and South Coast Railway reached the town in 1847.

Before 1834 horses and carriages passing between Portsmouth and Gosport had to go round through Fareham, though foot-passengers could of course cross the harbour by boat. In that year, however, a horse ferryboat was established, and in 1838 a steam-driven 'floating bridge' ferry of the kind recently invented by the Plymouth engineer James

---

* See below, pp. 119–125.

Rendel and already adopted by Southampton began to ply every half-hour to and from Point, where the current was so strong that an ordinary steam or sailing ferry-boat could not always make a crossing. This 'large and strange-looking structure, neither boat nor bridge and yet something of both', was flat-bottomed with no distinction of stem from stern and platforms at both ends to let down on the opposite beaches in order to take in and land foot-passengers, cattle, coaches, waggons, carts and even omnibuses. It had room for fifty vehicles and 500 passengers.[7]*

Though Southampton was now eclipsing Portsmouth in commercial importance, it still carried on coastal and some foreign trade, which had grown a little since the French wars. Its chief imports were wines and spirits, eggs, poultry, hares and partridges from France; timber, tar and hemp from the Baltic; grain; fruit and vegetables from the Channel Islands; and coal, sheep (from the Isle of Wight and the West of England) and granite coastally. It was also of some consequence for a time as a port of call; in 1840 nearly 100 homeward-bound ships, chiefly from the East and West Indies, landed their letter-bags at Spithead by pilot-boats, while 106 outward-bound vessels touched there to take in passengers. Southampton's superior facilities, however, especially after the opening of a railway to it from London in this same year, soon put paid to this. About 300 vessels belonged to the port, mostly employed in the coastal trade. After the failure of a project hatched in 1837 for the formation of docks, wharves and bonding warehouses on the shore of Langstone Harbour, entrance to which was to be effected by a canal from Southsea Castle past the backs of Lumps and Eastney Forts,† the Corporation as owners of the Camber promoted an improvement bill in 1839 under which they deepened the channel from the end of Point to the Town Quay and the projecting point of East Street, constituting a wet dock and surrounding it by wharves. Twenty years later they obtained another improvement act by virtue of which a dry dock costing £30,000 was built.[8]

In 1842 the Victoria Pier, projecting from the sea-wall near the Grand Parade at the foot of the High Street and approached by a glass-roofed colonnade, was constructed by a company of shareholders to increase the accommodation for passengers on the steam-packet service to and from the Isle of Wight which had been begun in 1817. For some years this pier was a popular resort, but its popularity declined rapidly after the opening of the first Clarence Pier in 1863, and in 1925 most of it was washed away by heavy seas.[9] In 1846–7 the Portsea or Albert Pier, projecting more than 1200 feet into the harbour from Portsea Hard, was built by the Harbour Pier Company to provide increased facilities for the landing of passengers and goods. The steamers of the

---

* The Floating Bridge ceased to function in 1958.
† This was only one of many abortive schemes for the development of Langstone Harbour.

Portsmouth and Ryde Steam Packet Company used it, but it was never a very flourishing undertaking, and when the railway was extended to the harbour in 1876 the Company was absorbed and the harbour viaduct and station occupied the site of the Pier.[10]

The first service of omnibuses, started in 1840, ran from Palmerston Road (then known as The Village) to North End by way of Southsea Common, the Quay, the Hard, Queen Street, the Lion Gate and along Commercial Road.[11]

The coming of the age of steam brought the railway to Portsmouth, though rather belatedly. The time-lag was due partly to physical circumstances; the barrier of Portsdown Hill, the fact that for all practical purposes the town was on an island, and the complications imposed by the old fortifications. There was also the effect of local rivalry with Southampton. One of the most important seaports of the country during the Middle Ages, Southampton had declined into a third-class port since the sixteenth century but had experienced after about 1740 a period of some celebrity as a spa, which at its height in the 1770s almost reached the first rank. Even so, it had been less than a quarter of the size of Portsmouth in 1801;* but now that its spa was dwindling away it had been quick to take advantage of the coming of steam-power and its application to transport and travel by land and sea. As early as 1831 a London and Southampton Railway Company had been formed, which completed its line from the capital in 1840, having in the meantime planned branches from what was to develop into Eastleigh to Portsmouth and Gosport, both *via* Fareham. The Portsmouth Corporation and 'owners and occupers of property', however, petitioned Parliament to reject the Company's bill for these latter lines, which instead of giving the town a direct route from London would leave it on a branch from Southampton's route and further from the capital in railway mileage than Southampton would be. In reply the Company diplomatically changed its name to London and South-Western and thereby mollified Portsmouth sufficiently for it to withdraw its opposition on the understanding that it would soon get a direct line of its own.

However at first only the branch through Fareham to Gosport was built, and opened in 1842; so that for five years after that the Portsmuthians who wanted to catch a train had to cross the harbour to do so. On the one hand their crossing was aided by the existence of the Floating Bridge, but on the other the Gosport railway terminus had had to be built outside the fortifications in order not to interfere with the town's defences, and was thus three-quarters of a mile from the landing-stage at Gosport Hard. The inconvenience to travellers in either direction was greatest at night, since the Floating Bridge did not run

---

* That is, of the borough. It was about the same size as old Portsmouth town.

then and returning passengers and anybody who wanted to catch the night mail train up had to make the crossing in an open boat. Moreover the effect on Portsmouth's trade of the lack of a direct railway was even more serious, for it was now that the Indiamen which in earlier years had landed letter-bags and passengers from Spithead ceased to do so, and much of the traffic with French ports also transferred itself to Southampton.[12]

Another result of the approach of the railway, even at this distance and with these handicaps, was that the Portsmouth mail coaches ceased to run. Hitherto there had been a dozen of them, to London, Oxford, Bristol and other places: the Royal Mail at 9.30 a.m. from the George Hotel to the White Horse Cellar in Piccadilly and the Bolt-in-Tun in Fleet Street; the Independent at ten o'clock from the Fountain for Charing Cross and the Spread Eagle in Gracechurch Street; the Tantivy in summer only, also from the Fountain but at noon, to the Bolt-in-Tun; the Rocket from the Rocket office at 61 High Street to the Belle Sauvage on Ludgate Hill; the Night Rocket starting on the same journey at 9 p.m. on weekdays; the Defiance to Brighton every day; the Union to Chichester on weekday afternoons; the Sovereign to Winchester thrice weekly; and so on; and of course the return services. Goods waggons or vans also lumbered (rather than ran) from the Van Office in Bath square to London and various other towns, taking anything from sixteen to twenty-four hours to cover the distance to the capital. They also carried passengers at cheaper rates but under more uncomfortable conditions than the stage-coaches (whose fares to London were 21s. inside and 12s. 6d. outside) and were patronised mainly by sailors.[13]

Meanwhile the London and Brighton Railway, which had reached Brighton in 1841, had absorbed a Brighton and Chichester Company that had thrown out an extension to Portsmouth, and a service of passenger trains from London *via* Brighton had therefore reached a terminus in Commercial Road by 1847. The London and South-Western was also now going ahead with its branch from Fareham *via* Cosham to Portsmouth; and since the line of the London, Brighton and South Coast (as the London and Brighton had now become) into Portsmouth was quite adequate to carry the traffic converging on Portsea Island from east and west, the LBSC and LSW came to an agreement to share it and own Cosham and Portsmouth stations jointly. In 1848 the link between Fareham and Cosham was completed, and a month later London and South-Western trains began to run into Portsmouth Terminus. Portsmuthians now had the choice of two routes to London, each of about 95 miles, *via* Eastleigh and Brighton respectively. This meant that the journey to the capital could be made in about three hours, whereas in the fastest days of the old coaching era even the mails were seven or eight hours on the road and other coaches took sixteen hours to cover the distance; while in the eighteenth century it had taken two days to reach London by road. Finally a Direct London and Portsmouth Company, which had built a line *via* Haslemere connecting the South-Western's Woking to Godalming branch with the LBSCR at Havant, was absorbed by the former, which began running trains into Portsmouth by this route in 1859.[14]

The upward leap of the borough's population in the 1840s and 1850s naturally manifested itself mainly in the suburbs, though the old town went on growing slightly till about 1863 and Portsea continued to expand substantially. But Kingston and North End increased by 45.6% in 1841–51 and 30.5% in 1851–61; while Landport and Southsea grew by 56.1% and 51.7% respectively during these twenty years. Landport spread along the main thoroughfares of Commercial Road and Lake Road and also along the other principal south-north route through Fratton and Buckland to the London road. Stamshaw and Copnor, too, showed accretions in the thirty years after about 1833. But the greatest urban spread was undoubtedly in Southsea and the southern part of Landport.[15]

During the '30s, '40s and '50s Southsea's growth was rapid. It spread in two distinct directions, north-eastward and south-eastward from Croxton Town. To the north it had linked up with Landport by the 1840s; while to the south the building of the villas in Clarence Park in the '50s brought it to the waterfront. The two expansions were quite different in character, showing between them a striking example of social stratification. That part of the northern spread which impinged on Landport was very like it, for here artisans mostly employed in the dockyard or in the many activities which supported it lived in long terraces laid out in the gridiron pattern of the day, with small general shops on the street corners. The southern part of this sector was much more in keeping with the general atmosphere developing in Southsea, with distinctly fewer shops and a fair sprinkling of the relatively well-to-do, though the houses were also in terraces and comparatively modest in size, mostly without front gardens. But it was the south-western expansion which gave Southsea its distinctive social and architectural flavour. Here the essential Southsea was created in these three decades, with substantial villas standing in their own grounds at the end of curving driveways, surrounded by brick walls and often by trees to ensure privacy.

'The creative genius behind the development of this . . . essential Southsea' was Thomas Ellis Owen. Born in 1804, he came to Southsea with his family in 1820, his father Jacob being clerk of the works to the Royal Engineers' Department. Articled at first to a London firm of architects, Thomas finished his education in Italy and in 1831 was made architect and surveyor to the Portsea Island General Cemetery Company, becoming a member of the Corporation at the same time. Almost at once he began to buy up plots of land to the east of Croxton Town, perhaps with his father's help, and by 1838 he had completed his first terrace, Queen's, and built a number of stuccoed villas. Ignoring those who prophesied bankruptcy for him, he went on buying land and building on it, preferring to let many of the houses he built rather than sell them; presumably because he could make more long-term profit thereby, since many people who wanted to spend a season in Southsea or retire there, and many naval or military officers who had to put in a term of duty and wished to make a temporary home for their families there, would rather rent a villa or a terrace house than buy one.

In 1847 Owen became Mayor of Portsmouth, and again in 1862; but soon after taking up his second term of office he died. To quote Dr Riley, as 'architect, builder, surveyor, property speculator, *rentier* and self-styled civil engineer, he spans the period up to the end of the 1850s almost like some feudal overlord, save that his influence was rather more subtle. . . . It was he who was responsible for the creation of Southsea's upper-middle-class enclave. It might have grown up without him, but it was he who gave it distinctiveness and therefore unity'; and what Mr. David Lloyd has called his 'strange and awkward villas' at least contributed much to create the select environment the Victorians loved. Not without justification, he has been called 'the man who built Southsea'.

In the '40s and '50s, then, Southsea spread towards Victoria Road on the one hand and what is now South Parade on the other. However this latter development, behind the Common, does not seem to have been due solely or even mainly to the growth of its reputation as a resort, but at this time rather to an influx of people coming to reside, permanently or for a period. After all, it was the railway more than any other means of transport which stimulated the holiday traffic, and the railway did not come till 1847. Till then, at least, Southsea was not a fully-fledged resort; and even though in the 1850's it became increasingly attractive to visitors its expansion towards South Parade was still apparently due less to this than to its growth as a suburb.

Its advantages had been enhanced by the draining and levelling of the Common between 1831 and 1843 (though the natural flora lingered for some time) and by the building of a promenade between the King's Rooms and Southsea Castle. This stemmed from a suggestion made by the Duke of Clarence in 1827, and when his son Lord Frederick Fitzclarence became Governor of Portsmouth in 1847 he gave strong support to the effort which the Corporation was then making to implement this idea. The work was completed in 1848 and the result became known as the Clarence Esplanade.[16]

To these new and relatively spacious developments Portsmouth and Portsea presented something of a contrast. Here much that was old, traditional and picturesque lingered, mixed up with a good deal that was noisy, violent and very often filthy and insanitary. The garrison, or detachments of it, drilled frequently on Southsea Common, watched by many interested spectators. Among these at a rather earlier period

(1812–14) had sometimes been a Mr John Dickens, a minor dockyard official, accompanied by his gay and pretty young wife and a nursemaid carrying his baby son Charles, whose earliest misty and rather precocious memories seem to have included being taken 'to see the soldiers'. In 1814, however, the family moved away to Chatham.

Every morning at daybreak a gun was fired from the walls of the old town and answered by the ships in the harbour. At sunset another was fired, and another at nine o'clock, after which the various military bands struck up and played on the fortifications for an hour. At ten they ended with 'God Save the Queen', after which no unauthorised person was allowed on the walls.[17] Even the Duke of Wellington, when taking a stroll on them in civilian clothes—it was he who inaugurated the practice of officers wearing mufti when not on duty—was turned off by a sentry who did not know him but was only doing his duty, as the Duke emphasised after quietly obeying.[18]

Another novelist, though a lesser one than Dickens, passed in his case the whole of his boyhood in this heart and centre of British naval life. Around 1840 George Meredith was growing up as a reserved and sensitive child in a house and tailor's establishment at 73 High Street which had been the leading naval outfitter's in Nelson's time under his strangely named grandfather Melchisedek, who was famed in his day as 'the Great Mel' and whom George afterwards portrayed along with the shop in his novel *Evan Harrington*.

It was at one or other of the Sally Ports close by that all seamen, officers and men alike, took their leave of the land or came ashore after a cruise and headed for their respective pleasures without delay. The officers' popular resorts were near at hand: the George Hotel for the seniors in rank and the Fountain for lieutenants, both in the High Street, and the Blue Posts* in Broad Street for the midshipmen. Here, as the coachman told Peter Simple in Captain Marryat's novel of that name, they 'left their chestesses, called for tea and toastesses, and sometimes forgot to pay for their breakfastesses'. The neighbourhood of Broad Street still kept much of the disreputable character that had overflowed into it from Point in the eighteenth century. Almost every house in it was a tavern, and for respectable townsfolk to stray into it after dark was to court all kinds of dangers; while in the neighbouring purlieus of East Street, Bathing Lane, Bath Square and Tower Street brothels proliferated.[19] Off the High Street, too, there were more of them, and in St Mary's (later rechristened Highbury) Street there was the Blue Bell music room, then rather notorious. These music rooms were the ancestors or embryos of the later music-halls and in their early days were almost always attached to public-houses. The standards of

---

* The original Blue Posts Inn, built in 1613, had large wooden pilasters, painted bright blue, flanking the entrances to the bar and the stable yard.

those in Portsmouth varied greatly. Many were of doubtful repute and were scenes of much disorder, especially when ships were being paid off; but some were very well conducted, among these being the Wiltshire Lamb and the Spread Eagle. The music room of the Blue Bell (to pursue its history a little further) was developed into a small music-hall in 1856 by a new licensee, William Brown. It continued to be patronised mainly by sailors, soldiers and their womenfolk, and fights were not infrequent; but in 1860 it was rebuilt as a larger and better-equipped establishment called the South of England Music Hall, where—in spite of the grandiose title—patrons could buy threepenny tokens at the door to be exchanged inside for two pints of beer.[20]

Within the old town there were still a few timber-framed houses, together with many low and rather picturesque gabled dwellings dating from the time when none were allowed to be higher than the town walls. At all the guardhouses, barracks, gates and posterns sentries kept watch day and night. The town gates were still closed at a certain hour at night, and to gain admission afterwards belated inhabitants had to give the countersign. Between the walls and those of Portsea the Mill Pond still spread its broad sheet of tidal water, across which ran a causeway and in the middle of which was an island that communicated with the causeway by an iron bridge. On the north or Portsea side was the Old Gun Wharf, dating from 1662; and on the south side, near the north end of the Camber, the New Gun Wharf built between 1797 and 1814. On both there were extensive ranges of storehouses, armories, smiths' workshops and so forth, belonging to the ordnance department of the Navy.[21]

The town walls were the playground, park and breathing-place for the children and the boulevards for their elders to walk on. Nursemaids took their charges to them every fine day. Little boys brought hoops and bowled them around them. They clambered about the bastions, peeped into the mouths of the cannon, sat on the gun-carriages and peered out through the embrasures, looking over into the moat below or playing at seeing an enemy beyond; or else they ran or rolled down the grassy slopes to the meadows where a clear area was still kept on which no houses might be built. In doing this they were trespassing and often fell foul of the special police for the walls, consisting of three or four notoriously short-tempered men called 'johnnies' who carried canes with which to 'warm' boys caught in the meadows or on the slopes.[22]

The reserved and instinctively 'superior' Georgie Meredith (nicknamed 'Gentleman Georgie' by his contemporaries) never stooped to take part in these games;[23] but among those who did was an eminently healthy and normal lad called Walter Besant, born eight years later than George, in 1836, as the fifth son of a merchant. Besant's novel *By Celia's Arbour*, published in 1878, and his autobiography written in 1900 both contain many passages of affectionate and indeed nostalgic description of early Victorian Portsmouth. To him and his playmates the King's Bastion, the last on the harbour side of the ramparts, was a special delight:

If you looked out over the ramparts you saw before you the whole of the most magnificent harbour in the world;* and if you looked through the embrasure of the wall you had a splendid framed picture—water for foreground, old ruined castle in middle distance, blue hill beyond, and above blue sky.

The 'old ruined castle' was of course that of Portchester, a favourite resort of the Besant family, to which they went every year for an excursion on which

we began by climbing to the roof of the keep, walking round the walls and looking into the chambers; this done, we had tea in one of the houses outside the walls. There was no tea like the Portchester tea; no bread like that of this happy village; no butter, no cakes, no shrimps comparable with theirs. After tea we walked home—seven miles.[24]

He also often rambled around Portsea as a boy, looking at 'the odd and pretty things which the sailors brought home and their wives put in their windows'; and of a character in his novel, a sailor's widow who was a washerwoman, he relates that:

Mrs Jeram was a weekly tenant in one of a row of small four-roomed houses. . . a broad blind court bounded on one side and at the end by the dockyard wall. It was. . . clean, and a very cathedral close for quietness. . . We† were quite respectable people. . . seafaring folk of course; and in every house was something strange from foreign parts. . . There were Japanese cabinets picked up in Chinese ports long before Japan was open [to Westerners]; there was curious carved wood and ivory work from Canton. These things were got during the Chinese War [of 1839–42]. And there was a public-house in a street hard by which was decorated, instead of with a red window-blind like other such establishments, with a splendid picture representing some of the episodes in that struggle. . . Then there were carved ostrich eggs; wonderful things from the Brazils in feathers; frail delicacies in coral from the Philippines. . . ; gruesome-looking cases from the West Indies containing centipedes, scorpions, beetles and tarantillas; . . . shells of all kinds. . . clubs, toma-hawks and other weapons. . . stuffed humming-birds and birds of paradise. There were live birds too—avvadavats, Java sparrows, love-birds, parroquets and parrots in plenty. . . The streets surrounding us were like our own, principally inhabited by mariners and their families, and presented similar characteristics, so that one moved about in a great

---

* When Sir Walter Besant, as by then he was, wrote this he had been a professor in Mauritius and seen something of the world and its harbours.
† Besant was here making one of his characters speak.

museum, open for public inspection during daylight, and free for all the world.[25]

Perhaps, even probably, Besant's rose-coloured recollections of his happy childhood, written thirty years afterwards, had a basis of fact. They are indeed one side of the picture. But they must not blind us to the very different and uglier aspects of Portsmouth and Portsea revealed by investigations which were being made at the very time when he was roaming round their streets and scrambling about the ramparts. Probably there were districts into which he never rambled, deterred by both parental warnings and a natural repugnance from squalor, and about which he knew little or nothing; courts that were very different from that in which he placed his 'Mrs Jeram', such as Messums, reached from a narrow back street below the town walls known as Prospect Row (which has now blossomed into Gunwharf Road) through a tunnel so contracted that it was called Squeeze-Gut Alley. Here 116 people lived, some of them in dark and damp cellars, with one privy between them and one standpipe which supplied water for perhaps ten minutes a day. For most purposes they used rainwater collected in butts outside their homes, or bought it at three-halfpence for two buckets from the travelling water-carts. Some sank wells in the muddy paths outside their doors. In Waterloo Street the mud lay permanently two feet deep, and in Paradise Row an open refuse pit was not cleared out for nineteen years. In the common lodging-houses like that in Cut-Throat Alley there might be found over sixty homeless beggars or sailors' wives crowded into one long low room, with beds almost touching, linen unwashed, windows rarely opened and walls never whitewashed. One lodging-house in Prospect Row was run by a man with so hideous and infectious a skin disease that the magistrates dared not send him to prison for a crime he had committed. Some schools were little more than daytime lodging-houses. In Upper Clarence Street 300 boys were packed into a room fifty feet long by thirty-six wide, with stone-flagged floors though many pupils went barefoot, and neither water nor drains laid on. In the now pleasant and even fashionable Oyster Street such little street and house drainage as there was ran into the Camber or the moats, which were rarely cleansed or flushed. The yards of St Thomas's Street swarmed with pigs which roamed in and out of the houses.[26]

Yet parts of Landport that had been hastily rushed up were as bad or even worse. To any sensitive nostrils the stench of the narrow crowded lanes on either side of the present Lake Road was almost intolerable. For want of proper refuse collection the inhabitants simply threw their ashes, garbage and filthy water into the streets or dug large ditches for them at the backs of the houses; with no street drainage, slimy puddles lay in every lane, overflowing on to the bare floors of the houses with every rainfall; with no water-closets, the one or two privies which each row of houses shared drained into cesspools that were rarely cleaned out and the contents of which seeped under the kitchen floors and into the well-water. In the hovels of Matrimony Row and the dens of Jacob's Ladder, with their walls half a brick thick and their eight feet by six feet kitchens slopping with liquid filth, the miserable inhabitants often shared a bed of straw and rags between three and four. It is very probable that young Besant had never entered this area and knew little about it.[27]

Such conditions as these, existing in parts of old Portsmouth, Portsea and Landport, could unhappily be matched in corresponding districts of many other English towns at this time. But here there were special circumstances which made things worse than in most of them. The military regulations which still closed the town gates at night from twelve till four kept within the walls the stinking night-waggons that twice or thrice a week had been cleansing at least some of the pits and cesspools. On warm nights the effluvia from these, as well as from the moats, the Mill Pond and the Camber, was particularly offensive. Point, by virtue of its proximity to all of these, was specially affected by this, which may account—taken in conjunction with its own lack of house drainage—for its having gained the ironical nickname of Spice Island. It was also said, with much understandable exaggeration, that in what were known as the metallic streets of the borough the sanitation was so bad that 'in Gold Street your sovereigns would tarnish; in Silver Street your shillings would turn blue; and in Copper Street your halfpence would turn to verdigris'.[28]

The development in the 1840s of a growing national interest in matters of sanitation and hygiene, however, prompted the Improvement Commissioners of Portsea in 1843 and of Portsmouth in 1847 to obtain new acts of Parliament giving them larger powers of lighting, paving, cleansing, watering and widening the streets, levying rates for these purposes, regulating hackney coaches and porters, and removing nuisances.[29] Under these acts they effected many improvements, though for the most part they were not such as to change very much the conditions described above. One thing they did, incidentally, was to abolish the Free Mart Fair originally granted to the town by Richard I's charter. Till the eighteenth century this had continued to be a useful and even considerable centre for the sale of woollen cloth, hardware and other manufactured goods; but it had now long outlived its usefulness and become latterly merely a pleasure fair, held on the Grand Parade at the foot of the High Street and all along that street, which had degenerated into a fortnight's saturnalia and pandemonium, to the annoyance and disgust of the soberer and more respectable of the townsfolk.[30]

These improvement acts of the '40s were closely followed by a crisis and a controversy centring about questions of public health and in particular water-supply. In 1808, nearly seventy years after Colonel Smith's abortive waterworks act of 1741 and almost half a century after his successor Peter Taylor had thrown in his hand,* two rival groups of promoters had emerged to compete for the supply of water to Portsmouth. One, incorporated in 1809 as the Portsea Island Waterworks Company, proposed to pipe their water from the White Swan Field springs,† while the other intended to supply water from springs in Farlington Marshes. Nearly thirty years of competition followed, with water also continuing to be supplied under the Improvement Commissioners' supervision by carters and from public and private wells. The two companies, however, provided between them only an inadequate supply, of poor quality, the Farlington Company's water sometimes containing mud and weeds (though a director claimed that the weeds improved it), while the Portsea Island Company's was very sandy. One customer complained that he had boiled some and 'put it into a clean Tea Pot purchased on purpose and after standing some time it came out a deep Orange Colour'. It was also subject to seasonal fluctuations in supply; and the Company was at a further disadvantage in that while its soft water was suitable for brewing porter the hard water of its Farlington rivals produced better ale, and most Portsmouth brewers were ale-men. Eventually the companies amalgamated in 1840 as the United Portsmouth, Portsea and Farlington Waterworks Company, which planned to supply the town wholly from Farlington. This United Company, however, could still cater only for a part of the market, and the remainder continued to depend on the sources under the Commissioners' control, the quality of whose water was now deteriorating.[31]

At this point the relation between the poor quality of Portsea Island water and the health of the town, which had not been generally recognised hitherto, was driven grimly and indeed tragically home by a cholera epidemic. The increasing national concern about urban conditions had led to the introduction into Parliament in 1847 of a Health of Towns Bill which proposed the setting up of a central Board of Health with powers of creating local boards on the petition of 10% of the ratepayers of a town or district and of enforcing their creation in places where the normal death-rate was above 23 per 1000. To this bill there was a widespread opposition from municipal authorities throughout the country, based on strong particularist and provincial feelings and repugnance at the idea of having local boards of health forced on them against their will. Since the average annual death-rate in Portsmouth between 1841 and 1847, even before the cholera came, was 25.37 per thousand, it was expected that if the Bill passed (which it did next year, becoming the Public Health Act of 1848) a board would be compulsorily established in the town; and the Portsea Commissioners protested in May 1847 that it would 'materially interfere with all local management

---

* See above, p. 75.
† See above, *ibid*.

and tend to increase Government patronage at the expense of rate-payers . . . [also] entirely supersede all existing locally elected repre-sentative boards'.

At the same time, however, they instructed their Sanitary Committee to report on the state of Portsea, which it did in February 1848. After describing the filthy condition of the courts, the state of the pavements and the shortcomings of the scavengers, the report stressed the defects of the water-supply. The Portsmouth Commissioners, for their part, appointed a surveyor and inspector of nuisances and an officer of health. But no effective remedy was introduced before the outbreak of cholera, which—as might be expected—spread rapidly through the worst districts of Landport and caused 152 deaths in the July and August of that year.[32]

The inhabitants of Landport, Kingston and Southsea, who had not even a board of commissioners to attempt preventive measures, now petitioned the newly created General Board of Health for an investigation into whether the state of the town warranted the creation of a local board; and Robert Rawlinson, a civil engineer who was a superintendent inspector of the Board, was sent down in December 1848 to carry it out.[33] In his report, presented in 1850, he found that

1. The Borough is not as healthy as it might be, because of ill-paved and unclean streets, imperfect privy accommodation, crowded courts and houses with large exposed middens and cesspools; and no adequate power for local government [i.e., sanitary administration] exists.
2. The excess of disease is distinctly traced to the undrained and crowded districts, deficient ventilation, absence of a full water supply and of sewers and drains generally.
3. The condition of the inhabitants could be improved by
   (a) a perfect system of street, court, yard, house drainage;
   (b) a constant and cheap supply of water. . . laid on to every house and yard to the superseding of all local wells and pumps;
   (c) the substitution of water-closets. . . for the. . . noxious privies and cesspools which exist, and by regular and systematic removal of all refuse at short intervals;
   (d) properly paved courts and passages, and by a regular system of washing and cleansing all courts, passages, slaughterhouses, footpaths and surface channels.[34]

Most of his report was devoted to emphasising how the lack of an effective sewage and drainage system endangered public health by polluting the water-supply—a point which was driven home, perhaps with some exaggeration, by the evidence of a local physician, Dr W. C. Engledue, founder of the Royal Portsmouth Hospital in 1846 and an enthusiastic sanitary reformer, who declared that:

At present the island of Portsea is one large cesspool, for there cannot be less than 16,000 cesspools daily permitting 30,000 gallons of urine to penetrate into the soil. Just reflect on the character of the well-water. . . which becomes mixed every year with 365 times 30,000 gallons of urine, to say nothing of other abominations.

After recommending a pumped system of house-drainage, Rawlinson went on to criticise the United Company's water-supply as bad in quality, deficient in quantity and excessive in price, and to urge the establishment of a waterworks, preferably municipally controlled, which would provide a constant service for all the inhabitants.[35]

His report was given added force by the fact that in the meantime the cholera had returned more virulently in July and August 1849. During these two months Portsmouth's doctors worked valiantly day and night, but all too often in vain. One of their difficulties was that no two of them agreed on the cause of cholera, how it was conveyed from person to person, or how to treat it. Some believed that it came from the tainted atmosphere; others that it was passed on by physical contact; others again blamed bad food or excessive drinking. The Improvement Commissioners warned the public against 'eating oysters, stale fish and unwholesome meats'. In St Thomas's churchyard the dead were buried in batches, usually before eight o'clock in the morning. The dockyard and other Government establishments were closed; business in the town was almost entirely at a standstill; and September 26 was set aside as a day of humiliation and prayer. In all over 800 people died of the disease.[36]

Nevertheless the committee appointed by the Portsea Commissioners to consider the report, still blinded by the fear of centralisation and alarmed by the probable cost of the proposals, did not advise its application. Instead they argued that the Commissioners already had sufficient powers to deal with the situation. The Borough Council took the opposite view, however, thus providing an example of the paralysing dichotomy between councils and improvement commissioners that was all too common then in municipal government. There followed several years of struggle, sometimes timid and half-hearted on the Council's part, between the 'clean party' who on the whole predominated in it and their opponents, whom they nicknamed 'the Muckabites' and who were headed by the Commissioners. In the course of this struggle various attempts to set up a local board of health were made by the former and blocked by the latter.[37]

However in 1855 the question of the water-supply was tackled in isolation and a committee of the Council reported in favour of its being municipally controlled; but consideration of its findings was postponed for a year, perhaps because the mayor of the moment was a leading figure in the United Water Company. Eventually, since the Council had thus failed to give a lead, Dr Engledue and two other members of it formed themselves into a provisional committee to force its hand. They consulted an engineer, who recommended buying out the United

Company and installing larger plant to supply the whole town from Farlington or from springs two or three miles further east at Bedhampton or Havant. These proposals were approved by the Council and an act was secured in 1857 empowering it to raise £80,000 for the purpose of buying out the Company and carrying out the proposed improvements. The transfer to the new Borough Waterworks Company was effected in the following year, and in due course it was able to provide a piped supply for almost all the inhabitants.[38]

Meanwhile in 1857 Landport and Southsea had obtained an improvement act of their own, creating yet a third body of commissioners for dealing with the parts of the borough not included in the acts of 1843 and 1847. They were granted extensive powers, but within a short time their inefficiency and mismanagement proved so great that the residents of Southsea took action which precipitated the end in Portsmouth of the antiquated system of administration by improvement commissioners (an end that had already occurred in many other places). A great meeting in 1863 at which there was even talk of cutting Southsea adrift from the rest of the borough was followed by the Borough Council's decision to adopt a recent Local Government Act that gave them power to abolish the Commissioners and take over their duties. This decision was upheld almost unanimously a few months later by a public meeting which was nevertheless one of the rowdiest ever yet held in Portsmouth, thanks to the behaviour of infuriated members of the expiring Landport and Southsea Board. The Commissioners' sanitary functions were transferred to a Portsmouth Local Government Board which became extinct in its turn in 1872 and was succeeded by an Urban Sanitary Authority afterwards merged into the Borough Council.[39]

Although there had been talk, at any rate at the time when Rawlinson's report was published, of the Corporation taking over the gas undertaking, the Gas Company continued in existence. It had been established in 1821, taking over some small and not very satisfactory gasworks established a few years earlier in Portsea by Barlow Brothers of London, and had afterwards set up rather larger works about half a mile north of the town on the Flathouse shore of the harbour.[40]

Various other amenities, material, spiritual and cultural, had been developed during the first half of the nineteenth century. A branch of the Bank of England had been established in Portsmouth in 1836, and by the middle of the century there were branches of the National Provincial Bank in Portsea and Landport, besides two private banks in Portsmouth and two in Portsea.[41] Twelve churches, over twenty nonconformist chapels (seven Baptist, six Independent, four Wesleyan, one Unitarian and several belonging to minor and obscurer sects), a Roman Catholic chapel and a Jewish synagogue existed by that time.[42] The Grammar School, after lapsing for many years rather earlier than most of its like did when the rising middle class showed little interest in a classical education, had been reopened in 1823, though it did not flourish until another forty years had passed.[43] Cultural institutions common to most sizeable towns at that time which functioned in Portsmouth included a Literary and Philosophical Society founded in 1815 and an Athenaeum which had begun in 1825 as a Mechanics' Institution for the diffusion of 'useful knowledge' to artisans but had changed its name when—as happened elsewhere—few of that class proved interested.[44] The theatre had experienced ups and downs, mostly the latter. John Collins, through whose influence Portsmouth had played a part of some importance in the theatrical history of the later eighteenth century, died in 1807. Under him it had been regarded as a good training-ground for actors, several Drury Lane stars having made their first appearances in the town, among them his brilliant but short-lived son Thomas. Collins's partner Davies had died ten years before him, and though his other son Stephen carried on the business side, the day-to-day running of the company passed to his son-in-law Henry Kelly and another leading member of it called Maxfield. For twenty years or so they struggled on with varying success against the difficulties caused by the post-Waterloo depression in Portsmouth, engaging London actors from time to time who drew good houses, in between which there were many poor ones. By 1829 the theatre had fallen into a state of disrepair, and in the following year it was bought by Thomas Owen as one of his earliest commercial ventures. Owen let it to Henry Hollingsworth,* but he was unable to get a licence and it reverted to Maxfield and resumed its vicissitudes. It was about this time that it was immortalised by Dickens in his novel *Nicholas Nickleby;* but on whom his seedy actor-manager Vincent Crummles was modelled has never been satisfactorily settled. In 1843 a rival theatre was opened in Landport by Thomas Hogg, who in the next year leased the old High Street theatre as well, running the two with the same company playing alternately at each. In 1850 Hogg went bankrupt and the Landport Theatre was sold off, while the other passed through the hands of at least four lessees in as many years until in 1854 it was sold to the War Office and demolished to make room for an extension to the Cambridge Barracks. In the same year, however, the Landport Hall, originally meant for meetings, assemblies and various forms of entertainment, was opened next door to the White Swan Inn and leased to a new arrival in the town, Henry Rutley, who had had experience of theatre management in London. Rutley converted the Hall into a Theatre Royal which opened in 1856 and ran it successfully, so that at the time of his death in 1874 it was in a flourishing condition.[45]

---

* See above, p. 96.

11. Mid-Victorian Portsmouth: war and rumours of war

The Crimean War of 1854–6, though in modern retrospect it has been condemned as needless, bloody and barren of results, was welcomed at the time by most Portsmuthians with the same enthusiasm as by most of their fellow-countrymen. Britain had not been involved in a European war for nearly forty years, and the country could in consequence almost be described as spoiling for a fight. Hence as events marched, or rather drifted, towards war in the opening weeks of 1854 the townsfolk watched the preparations for it with an approving interest that was nevertheless diluted by the fears of those many families of sailors and soldiers, naturally more numerous than in most other places, for whom it must mean the departure of their menfolk to danger and perhaps death.[1]

The review of the fleet which was to sail to the Baltic by Queen Victoria before its departure brought thousands upon thousands flocking into the town to join the townspeople in watching the spectacle. Then after the visitors had left again crowds of the inhabitants lined the streets day after day to cheer the regiments that marched from the barracks or the new railway station to embark in transports or war-steamers. A subscription was raised towards the Patriotic Fund set up by the Government to support the widows and orphans of the 'other ranks' who might be killed in action or (more frequently as the event proved) die of disease. Militia regiments, including Hampshire's, were brought into the town to replace in garrison the regular units which had gone overseas, and many militiamen enlisted into the line and in due course also found their way to the Crimea. Russian merchant ships appeared in the harbour as prizes, the first of them picked up on homeward voyages before they knew that their country was at war. The day of national humiliation and prayer which had been proclaimed was observed in a 'most becoming and respectful manner'; all Government establishments were closed, business was suspended, and all places of worship were duly attended by large congregations which listened to appropriate sermons. From the start of hostilities the victualling resources of the dockyard were worked day and night to meet the constant demand for provisions for the forces, but they still proved inadequate, so that a private baking firm in Southsea was called on to supplement them by preparing a large quantity of biscuit for the Navy.[2]

Then at the beginning of 1855 came the first batch of sick and wounded, together with women who had been allowed to accompany their husbands to the scene of war and were now mostly widows, and children who were mostly fatherless. The more urgent cases were taken to the military hospital in Portsea and the rest to a new auxiliary hospital which had been established near the Mill Dam, while the women and children were temporarily accommodated in the Clarence Barracks and then conveyed to their homes free of expense. From then on the townspeople had constantly before their eyes the saddening contrast between ships still leaving with men full of health and vigour and others returning with men maimed or broken in health. At last the war came to an end and even the scenes of enthusiasm which had marked the first departure of the Baltic Fleet were surpassed by those which celebrated the return to peace. Though the Navy had accomplished disappointingly little in either the Baltic or the Black Sea, so many people flocked to Portsmouth to see the victory review that the cost of accommodation in the town rose to what for those days were fantastic figures. Houses were temporarily at the disposal of the highest bidder, and £50 was merely a modest charge for two nights' lodging for a family of three; while most of those who arrived hopefully on the evening before the review could not find a hole or corner in which to sleep at any price.[3]

The war, bringing Britain and France together in alliance against Russia, had for the time being removed the fear of a French invasion.[4] This fear had its origin in the fact that it was France rather than Britain which was taking the lead in the application of steam-power to naval warfare and in the other new developments which were transforming the navies of the mid-nineteenth century. At the same time the interests of the two countries were clashing repeatedly in various parts of the world and thus causing strained relations in spite of periods of reconciliation and even co-operation; and since Britain's growing commercial and colonial commitments brought with them the need for ships to be permanently stationed in many distant seas, so that the number available in home waters was sometimes surprisingly small, it was feared that France might avail herself of her lead in steam-power to seek revenge for Trafalgar and Waterloo by a sudden blow at Britain's coasts. There had been minor panics on this score in 1845–7 and again in 1851–2 when Napoleon's nephew Louis Napoleon came to power in France and then assumed the title of Emperor; and the Crimean War was hardly over before fears and friction grew again, despite his professions of friendship for Britain, which are now recognised to have been sincere.

In 1858–9 this growing alarm was intensified by the implications of two inventions, one British and one French, that coincided with it—the Armstrong gun and the ironclad warship. The former greatly increased the range and penetrative power of heavy artillery; in fact experts estimated (though perhaps with some exaggeration) that its range had been doubled, from a maximum of 4,000 yards to 8,000. For a short time Britain alone would have this gun, but it had to be assumed that other nations would soon possess its like. This would mean, if their estimated range was anywhere near the truth, that British dockyards, arsenals and harbours could be bombarded from positions hitherto undefended, without the attackers being seriously hampered by any of the defensive works then existing or in course of construction. In particular it meant, or seemed to mean, that all Portsmouth's fortifications, actual and projected, had been made obsolete or inadequate almost overnight.

Together with Gosport, whose defences had been considerably strengthened in the later eighteenth century, Portsmouth and Portsea constituted three walled and (it had hitherto been thought) strongly defended towns bordering the mouth of Portsmouth Harbour. They were in fact the only completely walled towns in England, apart from Berwick-on-Tweed, to survive as such beyond the Middle Ages. Various improvements had also been added to the defences during the last sixty or seventy years. Fort Cumberland had been entirely rebuilt between 1789 and 1794, making it 'perhaps the most impressive piece of eighteenth-century defensive architecture' remaining in the country.* Successive additions had been made to Southsea Castle, though latterly it had been used mainly as a military prison; and the moat outside the town ramparts had been deepened in 1820.[5] In 1851–2 the batteries protecting the harbour mouth had been strengthened, two new ones erected at Browndown to cover the shores of Stokes Bay, and two forts—Gomer, west of Alverstoke, and Elson on the upper part of the western side of Portsmouth Harbour—had been begun in advance of Gosport and on either side of its peninsula. Then in 1858 it was decided to build three more forts between these two and to reconstruct the Hilsea Lines in earth and brick and provide them with a moat, in a style still recognisably in the tradition of De Gomme and his successors.

The greatly increased range of heavy artillery, however, would now make it possible for the dockyard and harbour to be bombarded from Portsdown Hill 7,000 yards away or from some point beyond the Gomer-Elson line. This of course presupposed that a considerable enemy force could establish itself ashore and in rear of Portsmouth; but many of the French invasion plans of the eighteenth century—of which the British higher command and rudimentary intelligence service had some retrospective knowledge—had envisaged just such a landward attack on Portsmouth after a sudden descent on the west Sussex coast.

---

* The fact that convict labour had been mainly used for the rebuilding of Fort Cumberland had prompted the historian Edward Gibbon to improvise the following couplet:
  'To raise this bulwark at enormous price
  The head of folly used the hand of vice',
while being shown over it.

Even without a landing the range of the new guns would enable an enemy fleet to shell the dockyard if it could penetrate the outer fringes of Spithead.

The second alarming development, the evolution of the ironclad, was one in which Britain had at first led the way, only to fall behind more recently when France embarked on the construction of a squadron of armoured steam frigates or corvettes which she intended to complete by 1861. A committee set up in Britain in consequence of this in December 1858 reported alarmingly four months later on the relative naval strength of the two countries. Britain's total steam navy was much larger than France's but her preponderance was entirely in the smaller vessels, so that in capital ships suited to modern warfare France was at the moment numerically equal. Moreover there were two other vitally important considerations. Since a greater proportion of Britain's ships were scattered in distant seas, she was actually inferior in European waters; and on top of this the committee's figures did not include France's new armoured squadron, which it was reckoned would make wooden-hulled battleships, even though fitted with steam propulsion (the best that Britain possessed as yet), as obsolete as these had made sail of the line. The first of these vessels, *La Gloire*, was indeed launched soon afterwards, but it was the committee's report and not her launching that shocked the country and stimulated the Admiralty and the Government into almost feverish activity.

Britain's reply to the challenge, or supposed challenge, from France was threefold—the volunteer movement, the outbuilding of the French ironclads by a greater and more sustained effort than France had the resources to keep up, and the most thorough overhauling of the national defences that had ever yet been undertaken.

The volunteer movement which thus arose in 1859, however, did not in Portsmouth reach the proportions that it attained in many other places, never attracting even in its early years of enthusiasm more than 800 men out of a civilian population of over 70,000. The reason was probably that since it was a large garrison town the military were so much an everyday sight that a uniform did not have the romantic attraction for a Portsmuthian that it possessed elsewhere; while on the other hand they were so sharply divided from the civilians, sometimes (at least) so convinced of their superiority to them, and probably in most cases so doubtful or scornful of the military value of volunteers that many people may have been deterred from enrolling by feeling that if they did so they would be looked down on more than ever for feebly trying to imitate their betters. A further handicap—though this was shared with many other towns—was that three mutually jealous corps were formed instead of one. Volunteer units were in any case small at first, since it was originally a deliberate policy that they should be trained either as sharpshooting riflemen who could act as auxiliaries to the regulars and milltia in the field, or as garrison artillerymen. But in

Portsmouth there were special local circumstances which combined with two problems common to volunteer corps in general, those of choosing a uniform and selecting officers, to produce this inter-unit jealousy.

The first corps to be formed, the Fifth Hampshire Rifles, had secured Sir David Cunynghame, a retired officer of the 12th. Lancers who lived locally, as their commanding officer, and had appointed a committee to devise a uniform. The Marquis of Winchester, however, who as Lord-Lieutenant of Hampshire had (like his fellow lords-lieutenant in other shires) been invested by the War Office with authority over the volunteer units of his county, wished to make them all wear an ash-coloured uniform, turned up with green, of his own invention. Sir David promptly resigned on the ground that no former lancer officer could be seen in such a get-up and was succeeded by a retired Indian army major who did not share his feelings. Most of the Fifth, perhaps influenced by their grandfathers' stories of what the Golden Goldfinches had worn sixty years before, also thought the proposed uniform very unmilitary, but since the only way of getting the corps started was to wear it they eventually agreed to do so. Soon afterwards, however, about half of them decided that they would rather be artillerymen and seceded to form the 2nd. Hampshire Volunteer Artillery Corps under Major Samuel Hill the town barrack-master. Although the secessionists disclaimed any idea of opposition to the Fifth an understandable jealousy persisted for some time between the two corps.[6]

The third unit was formed a little later in the dockyard, where two volunteer corps had existed previously for a few years after the first invasion scare of 1845–7—an infantry battalion under the command of the Master Shipwright and an artillery corps under the Master Attendant. Though these totalled 1,870 men when they were formed they had faded out of existence ten years later. In 1860, however, a Third Hampshire Volunteer Artillery Corps was established in the yard. The question of a commanding officer then arose. Volunteer officers could be granted their commissions only on the Lord-Lieutenant's recommendation, but the practice had grown up of the members of a corps electing a candidate and recommending him to the Lord-Lieutenant, who usually accepted him. Since there was already a precedent for the commandant being chosen from within the yard, and since the dockyard men preferred to be commanded by someone who understood them and whom they knew and liked, they chose Assistant Master Shipwright Sturdee, who duly became captain-commandant. But soon there came a further problem. The volunteer rank of an officer commanding a corps depended on its numbers, and since the 3rd. Hampshire V.A.C. soon became the largest in the town Sturdee rose quickly to be a lieutenant-colonel, outranking Major Hill. Worse still, the Hampshire corps, like those of other counties, were presently grouped into rifle battalions and a brigade of artillery. Sturdee as the senior in rank of the three officers commanding volunteer artillery corps in the county automatically received command of the brigade, whereupon Hall in his turn resigned on the ground that as an officer who had seen much active service he could not take orders from a man who was to all intents and purposes a civilian. His action met with a good deal of criticism as reflecting an attitude at variance with the proper volunteer spirit, though it was not he but the Portsmouth doctor who was the corps' surgeon who referred contemptuously to Sturdee as 'a carpenter'.[7]

Meanwhile the question of the national defences had been referred to a royal commission which was instructed to begin its work by considering the defence of Portsmouth, as being both the most important British naval base and the place where the greatest difficulties existed. Its recommendations, when modified by a Defence Committee afterwards appointed under the Commander-in-Chief, the Duke of Cambridge (who was also the Queen's cousin), were that six forts should be constructed along the crest of Portsdown Hill—Wallington, Nelson, Southwick, Widley, Purbrook and Farlington Redoubt; a new advanced line of three forts (of which only one, Fort Fareham, ever materialised) should be built on the Gosport peninsula still further forward than the Gomer-Elson line; and for the protection of Spithead forts should be erected on the shoals known as Nomansland, Horse Sand and Sturbridge.

The Portsdown forts and Fort Fareham, though rather delayed by alterations of scale and plan and by building difficulties met with at Fort Wallington, which was built partly on greasy and slippery clay, were finished by 1868. The owner of Portsdown Hill, Thomas Thistlethwaite of Southwick Park, received £95,200 compensation for 900 acres of land which had been taken over plus another 1,000 acres over which clearance rights had been obtained in order to improve the field of fire, and for the general damage to the amenities of his estate by the loss of its 'grand commanding feature'. The two ladies whose tea-gardens on the hill had for many years been the goal of country excursions from Portsmouth and elsewhere were also paid compensation. The Spithead forts met with still greater difficulties and experienced longer delays. It became evident that a good foundation could not be obtained on Sturbridge Shoal without incalculable expense, and Spit Bank was substituted. Then, since an enemy who had passed the forts at Nomansland and Horse Sand might keep so far over towards the Isle of Wight as to be out of effective range from Portsea Island, a small fort was begun on Ryde Sand. But after much time had been spent on this it proved as unsuitable a location as Sturbridge had been, and it was decided instead to build a small work near the edge of the shoals in front of St Helen's Point, close to the island shore. Furthermore the long period over which construction stretched out led again to changes of scale and style, so that it was not till 1880 that all four forts were finished. The combination of the Portsdown and Spithead forts constituted the last and most extensive ring fortification to be built around any European city in the nineteenth century, and for a time Portsmouth became one of the most strongly defended places in the world.

Long before this a *rapprochement*, though a rather temporary one, had taken place between Britain and France, and a generation which therefore saw no need for the forts gave them the nickname of 'Palmerston's Folly' by which they continued to be known. The implication was that Lord Palmerston, who was prime minister when their construction was decided on, had in a moment of panic committed a needless extravagance in taking such elaborate precautions against what was by then believed to have been a purely imaginary peril of attack. But while on the one hand there can be no doubt that the alarm which led to their building was exaggerated, on the other hand it was both more natural and less groundless than has generally been realised. Perhaps Napoleon III could never have been pushed into war with Britain, even when ageing and broken in health, as he was dragged towards war with Prussia in 1870. But Palmerston and his colleagues were right to remember and remind others that it was unsafe to assume that he would always be master in his own house and that in any case he was not immortal. He might have died earlier than he did and left the government of France to pass into hands more hostile to Britain, in which case an incident or a chain of incidents and misunderstandings might have led to war. It was in fact war by misadventure, of which the Crimean War could be reckoned a very recent example, that Palmerston regarded as the danger most to be guarded against. It may at least be questioned whether the measures he took to do so would not have been more justly called 'Palmerston's Prudence'.*

The more recent of the pre-existing fortifications—Fort Cumberland, Southsea Castle, Forts Blockhouse and Monckton, the Gomer-Elson line and the Hilsea Lines—were approved by the Defences Commission and incorporated into the Palmerstonian scheme as a second line of defence. But the old town ramparts round Portsmouth and Portsea had now become redundant, and in the 1870s they were first of all pierced by the extensions of the railway to the harbour and into the dockyard and then demolished; except that the seaward line of Portsmouth's walls, from the King's Bastion at the south-east corner to the Square Tower together with Point Battery, was retained as still providing important sites for guns covering the immediate approaches to the harbour, and was used as part of the town's defences up to and throughout the 1939–45 war. Four of the old town gates also survived, one (the Landport) *in situ* though in an incongruous setting, while the others were re-erected elsewhere: King James's Gate in the Royal Naval Barracks

---

* Within a few years of the completion of the forts, however, the further development of artillery was already leading military experts to criticise, not the building of them, but the nature of their construction, which they claimed had rapidly made them obsolete.

(whence its remnants were later removed again to the left-hand side of Burnaby Road, leading into the United Services Officers' Recreation Ground); the Lion Gate in the dockyard, where it was built into the base of the Semaphore Tower; and the other Portsea town gate, the Unicorn, as the entrance into the dockyard from Flathouse Road. The sites of the vanished ramparts and of the Mill Pond which was filled in at the same time were used for barracks, Service recreation grounds, a public park (the Victoria Park, opened in 1880) and further extension of the dockyard.[8]

In more recent times, after the Second World War, the Portsdown forts have met with diverse fates. Fort Nelson stands empty at the moment, Southwick has become an extensive radar establishment, Widley is owned by the Corporation and has been thrown open to the public, Purbrook has also been taken over by it and is at present (1973) being worked on, Farlington is derelict and Wallington was bought in 1961 for use as a storage depot and partly demolished. The Solent forts, which had been manned during the 1939–45 war, still belong to the Ministry of Defence, which in 1963 considered selling them. The City Council, however, alerted by some of the suggestions for their use which were being bandied about to the possibility of their being plastered with enormous advertisements and the like, managed to prevail on the Ministry to drop the idea for the time being.[9]

12. Steady advance, 1860–1914

In 1860 the population of the borough of Portsmouth was about 80,000, of whom between 10,000 and 11,000 lived in the old town, approximately 17,000 in Portsea, and nearly all the rest in Landport, Kingston and Southsea. These last three now extended in one continuous mass of buildings along the east side of the then still existing fortifications of Portsmouth and Portsea, southwards to Southsea Castle, northwards nearly to Tipner and Hilsea, and eastwards to Fratton and Buckland, beyond which lay the village of Copnor. The whole could be considered as a single town about two and a half miles in length from north to south and one and a half in breadth from east to west. Within it the balance was shifting. Old Portsmouth was becoming something of a backwater, and had been called little more than an appendage to the Camber with its limited trade and to the barracks of the two Services. In the next twenty years or so its population shrank considerably. Even after its ramparts had been removed and the Mill Pond filled in, the new barracks and sports fields that took their places still cut it off from the rest of the growing city. The population of Portsea also declined, although it was the dockyard quarter and in the age of steam the dockyard was increasing rapidly; for it was mostly Landport and to a less extent a part of Southsea that took the overspill of the dockyard workers. Already in 1871 the census report commented on 'the gradual removal of residents from the business centres of Portsmouth and Portsea to the modern suburbs outside the walls'. Many former dwelling-houses in the two older towns were being converted into business premises, but otherwise Portsmouth and Portsea changed comparatively little in the next forty years or so and, apart from their public buildings, could almost be said to be stagnating.[1]

Meanwhile Landport, Kingston and Southsea continued to grow apace, and it was their increase that caused the upsurge of the total population of the borough, from 94,329 in 1861 to 113,569 in 1871; 127,989 in 1881 and 159,251 in 1891.[2] Landport, the largest of the three, was now replacing old Portsmouth as the focal point of the urban area.

Steadily the areas between Arundel Street and the railway and between Lake Road and Kingston Crescent were filled in; the stretch of Landport (later renamed Commercial) Road north of the railway developed into an important shopping centre; and the building of a magnificent new Town Hall in 1886–90 made it the municipal centre as well.[3]

Southsea continued to develop as the fashionable quarter and as a resort. But here a distinction must be made. It was in its western and perhaps its central areas that the characteristic features of a Victorian seaside resort developed—piers, hotels, ornamental gardens and a railway line. In addition to these the growth of the core of upper-middle-class Southsea between 1860 and about 1885 consisted of the filling in of existing roads with villas, especially along and behind South Parade. In the 1860s there was a spate of hotel building: the Pier Hotel, the Beach Mansions, the Sandringham, the Grosvenor, the Esplanade—names redolent of Victorian seaside respectability. In 1861 Clarence Pier was opened near the King's Rooms, T-shaped to allow two paddle-steamers to berth there at the same time and enable it to carry the through traffic for the Isle of Wight, which it did until Portsmouth Harbour Station was built in 1876. This traffic to the Island was now growing considerably, thanks both to the coming of the railway to Portsmouth and the increasing popularity of family holidays at the seaside among the middle class. At first passengers travelled from the Landport (or Town) railway station to Clarence Pier by horse-bus, but in 1865 a horse-tram service began, the trams running directly on to the now enlarged pier.[4] In 1874 this became a centre of controversy and even disturbance when the Pier Company got permission from the Admiralty and War Office to close the road between it and the nearby Esplanade Hotel. The townsfolk resented this infringement of their rights, and a party of them marched on the barricade, broke it down, and burnt it on the beach. For days crowds milled around the Pier, and when they began to get out of hand troops were called in. Eventually the order was rescinded and the road opened again.[5]

A second and much longer pier was built in 1879 at South Parade, its promoters optimistically hoping that it also could be made a point of departure for the Isle of Wight. It was considered more fashionable than Clarence Pier, but was less convenient and probably less profitable, since the other was much closer to most of the hotels and apartment-houses. In 1904 this first South Parade Pier was destroyed by fire, whereupon the Corporation took over the site and rebuilt it in 1908.

More than thirty years earlier the Council had begun to think of providing additional facilities on the Common for summer visitors, but had been hampered at first because it was still War Department property. In 1870 a seawall had been built to the east of Southsea Castle, and in 1878 seventeen acres of land at Lumps Fort had been leased from the Government for recreational purposes; but it was only after a lease of the whole of the rest of the Common had been obtained in 1884 that it became possible to develop it fully. Although it had been drained and mostly levelled in the 1830s and early 1840s its eastern part had remained a haunt of wildfowl, as is implied by its name of Craneswater which was transferred as Craneswater Park to a district of genteel houses that began to be developed in 1877 on some of its more inland area. Between this and the sea lay a dismal-looking depression strewn with rusty tins, mouldy rubbish and other offensive objects, which after it had passed into the hands of the Corporation was converted into an ornamental Canoe Lake in 1886. These developments contributed largely to create a second focal point for Southsea at South Parade Pier. Meanwhile after the establishment of Morant's and Handley's department stores in 1867 Palmerston, Osborne and Marmion Roads became a select shopping district where high-class tailors, jewellers, wine merchants, watchmakers and photographers competed for the patronage of the well-to-do families and visitors. Of Palmerston Road a guide-book of about 1890 commented that it was 'a popular and fashionable parade-ground with a constant stream of the *élite* of Southsea and the walk of cultivated society'.

Eastward expansion of the built-up area of Southsea had continued, though well back of the beach because of the obstacles provided by Craneswater, Lumps Fort and Eastney Barracks (completed in 1867). Here row after row of artisan terraces were built until soon after the turn of the century east Southsea had reached its physical limits. There were a number of small apartment-houses in this district for people who wanted cheap seaside holidays, but the greater part of it remained residential, since the chief cause of its rapid growth during these years was the expansion of the dockyard. Construction workers, dockyard employees and sailors' families were all seeking houses at this time, and it was the demand for them rather than Southsea's progress as a resort that was the reason for so much new building in this region. By contrast the area facing the Common to the west of South Parade Pier had become a mature and select seaside resort by the end of the century—'a gentlemanly place', as another guide-book put it complacently in 1896.[6]

A branch railway to Southsea was one of the only two public railway developments of any importance to take place on Portsea Island after 1860, the other and more lasting one being the extension of the main line from the Town Station in Commercial Road to the harbour, already mentioned.* The Southsea line, opened in 1885, ran for one and a quarter miles from a station built at Fratton (and called Fratton and Southsea between 1905 and 1921) to a terminus in Granada Road. It operated till 1914, but never at a profit, for it was as inconvenient as it was slow, not being long enough to make it worthwhile for many local

---

* There was also a branch line, not open to the public, into the dockyard from near the Town Station.

passengers to betake themselves to either end. Only during the last ten years of its existence were any intermediate stopping-places provided. Its sole justification would have been to carry sufficient long-distance passengers to and from Southsea, but the connections at Fratton were often so leisurely that such people usually preferred to leave or join the train there or at Portsmouth Town and use a tram for the rest of their journey. At the outbreak of the first world war traffic on the line ceased, and in 1923 it was abandoned.[7]

The development of the dockyard, though very considerable as a whole, was not continuous during this period, since at first there were fluctuations. The early years of the ironclad from 1863 to 1875 were still a period of transition and uncertainty in naval architecture and technology, and since Government policy tended to favour land fortifications rather than to listen to the 'Blue Water School'* shipbuilding in the yard was somewhat restricted; though the *Devastation*, a mastless warship launched in 1870 which was the first ironclad to be built there, marked a definite stage in the advance to the modern battleship. Nevertheless 1,500 men had been summarily discharged from the dockyard in 1868, and as most of them were unable to find other work their condition became so pitiable that a fund was raised in the following year to assist those who wished to emigrate to Canada with their families. About this time, however, a great expansion of the yard began, with many additional dry docks, large enclosed basins and 'buildings of great size and sometimes of external splendour', so that its area was almost tripled, from 116 to 300 acres. The age of steam was now gathering momentum. Facilities for sailing ships were almost entirely swept away; the rigging-house, sail-loft and ropehouse were adapted for other purposes; and many new workshops and storehouses were built to meet the needs of steam and an ironclad fleet. The demolition of Portsea's fortifications provided part of the extra land required, and more was obtained by reclamation from the mudlands. The mud excavated from these was used to extend Whale Island in the upper harbour. Before 1845 this had been covered at every spring tide, but by successive deposits of spoil from the large steam basin which was then under construction it had been raised ten or fifteen feet above sea-level, and in 1861 the Government had bought it from the Corporation for £1,000. It was now increased to about six times its former size, and in 1891 the Navy's chief gunnery school was transferred to it from the hulks *Excellent*, *Boyne* and *Charlotte*, which had previously lain in the harbour, and was henceforth known as H.M.S. *Excellent*.[8]

After 1875 the tempo of naval shipbuilding quickened again, and during the last quarter of the century the yard played a leading part in the construction and development of the pre-*Dreadnought* battleships.

---

* The senior naval officers and navalist writers who urged reliance on the Navy for the protection of the British Isles.

The total tonnage launched there in the '80s was 47,450, rising to 104,665 tons in the '90s, for though fewer vessels were built in each successive decade the aggregate tonnage increased because of the growing size of warships. Between 1888 and 1912 fifteen acres of the built-up area of Portsea were taken into the yard; the tonnage launched between 1900 and 1909 mounted to 136,810; and outstanding among the ships launched was the *Dreadnought* itself, built in record time in 1905–6, the first all-big-gun warship, which opened a new epoch in battleship construction. From then till 1921 the dockyard continued to play the major part among naval yards in the development and building of capital ships. It is true that private yards with larger building slips and better facilities produced between them two-thirds of the dreadnoughts of this era, but Portsmouth built more than any other single yard.[9]

It was not only the dockyard which was extended during this period, for the boundaries of the county borough (as it had become in 1888) were enlarged to include the whole of Portsea Island by taking in Great Salterns in 1895 and Hilsea in 1904. By 1911 the population, which had been 188,133 in 1901, had risen to 231,141.[10] Further barrack accommodation also became necessary; and in addition to the Eastney Barracks for the Royal Marines already mentioned, the Victoria Barracks adjoining Southsea Common were built in the early '80s and the Royal Naval Barracks on the site of the older Anglesea Barracks in 1899–1903. Since the Naval Barracks also displaced the former military hospital in Lion Terrace, Portsea, the Alexandra Military Hospital was built at Cosham on the southern slopes of Portsdown Hill and opened in 1908.[11] On the civilian side new public buildings included a much larger gaol, on a site acquired in 1903 by the Corporation at Milton, where a mental hospital had also been established in 1879, the borough's mental patients having been previously sent to asylums in the county.[12] On a happier note, two developments in the field of higher and technical education followed each other in quick succession in 1907–8; the opening of a day training college for women teachers and a Municipal (Technical) College, an increasing number of whose students sat for the external degrees of London University.[13] The Grammar School, which had experienced another period of decline and virtual extinction, was resuscitated in 1875 and rapidly began to flourish. By 1878 it had outgrown its old building in Penny Street and moved to a new one on ground at the corner of Cambridge Road and St George's Road which the demolition of the ramparts had made available. In 1926 it moved again to occupy the former Cambridge Barracks in High Street near by.[14]

Towards the end of the century the Corporation, like others elsewhere, began to extend its functions to providing or taking over public amenities. In 1891 it decided to introduce electric lighting into the borough, though it was only the Mayor's casting vote which prevented this from being left to a private company;[15] and in 1898 it took over the horse-tramways by compulsory purchase*. Their development had been slow. Although the service already mentioned† had been opened between the Town Railway Station and Clarence Pier in 1866, there had been much opposition to overcome before the next step could be taken by the construction of a line from the Floating Bridge to Edinburgh Road at the beginning of the '70s; and for years after that residents in some of Southsea's more exclusive streets continued to object to any further extension that might trespass upon their quiet respectability. Their chief complaints were of the noise of the horses' hoofs, 'the rude staring of the passengers who would occupy the cheap seats on the top deck', and the outrage of running trams on the Sabbath.[16]

In 1910 the Corporation embarked on its first essay in slum-clearance and town planning with the acquisition of 200 houses in a slum area described as 'a sink of iniquity' and their replacement by a wide tree-lined street of forty-six houses of a relatively modern type for artisans.[17]

The town's longest-lived newspaper, the *Hampshire Telegraph*, had flourished steadily since its foundation in 1799. In the early years of the nineteenth century several attempts had been made to establish other journals, but all had ended in failure until in 1850 the *Portsmouth Times* appeared and ran in friendly rivalry with the *Telegraph* until it was absorbed by it in 1928. Another competitor, the *Hampshire Post*, started in 1874, had met the same end in 1913. All these were weeklies. The first daily—or rather, evening—paper, the *Evening News*, was launched in a very modest way in 1877. In 1884 it found a formidable rival in the *Evening Mail* (later renamed the *Southern Daily Mail*), but the two joined forces in 1905 under the older paper's name. In 1932 a company with the title of Portsmouth Newspapers, Limited, was formed to take over both the *News* and the *Telegraph*.[18]

In the ecclesiastical sphere there were two notable occurrences in the later years of the century; the rebuilding of St Mary's Church at Kingston and the meteoric career in Portsmouth of Father Robert Dolling. The medieval St Mary's had been replaced in 1843 by a building to the design of Thomas Owen of Southsea, but with the greatly increased vitality of church life in the parish under Canon Edgar Jacob this in turn had become inadequate by 1883. Canon Jacob turned to the distinguished architect Sir Arthur Blomfield, whose brother happened to be his senior curate, for the building of a much bigger

---

* In 1920 bus services were begun on routes and to areas not served by the trams, and were rapidly extended. In 1934 trolley-buses began to be substituted for trams, and in 1936 the last tram was withdrawn. (Art. on Portsmouth in *Municipal Journal*, 1 July 1955, p. 1771).

† See above, p. 127.

church; but the size of Blomfield's estimate gave the Vicar food for anxious thought until one day he met in the train W. H. Smith, a cabinet minister and son of the founder of the famous firm of bookstall stationers, and poured out his worries to him. Smith proved a *deus ex machina* and a munificent benefactor, providing well over half the cost of the new church between 1884 and 1889. In the decades that followed St Mary's became noted throughout the Anglican world for its system of parochial organisation and pastoral care. It was also nicknamed 'the nest of bishops', since not only did Canon Jacob become Bishop of Newcastle and afterwards of St Albans, but two of his successors rose to be archbishops—Cosmo Gordon Lang, of York and then of Canterbury, and C. F. Garbett, of York—while several curates reached episcopal rank.[19]

A year before Canon Jacob decided to rebuild St Mary's, the Winchester College Mission was established in the poorest and slummiest part of Landport near the dockyard. This area was described by one of the Mission clergy as a curious little island in the great town of Portsmouth,[20] and was an irregular square bounded by the dockyard wall, Unicorn and Edinburgh Roads, and Commercial Road which was now said to be the busiest street in the south of England outside London and was sometimes called 'the Navy's Regent Street'.

Day and night it was full of bustle—it was without doubt the pulse of the port, albeit a feverish one. The bigger shops were open until midnight; the smaller ones all night. There were... peep-shows, flea circuses, exhibitions of the fattest woman in the world, the smallest, the hairiest, the boy with two heads, the boy with three legs—in fact all the excitement and grotesqueness of life.[21]

The district enclosed within these bounds was still a mass of small and overcrowded dwellings, with old red-tiled roofs and interiors that often resembled ships' cabins—'a sort of municipal Cinderella sitting in rags amid its better cared-for sisters of the borough'.[22] It had 51 public-houses, most of them with music rooms of a low type, and many houses of ill-fame, though there were several streets whose inhabitants were decent and well-behaved. Through the area there ran like an axis Charlotte Street, formerly nicknamed 'Bloody Row' from the number of butchers' shops in it and slaughter-houses behind it, the latter of which could still be smelt from afar off. At night, especially on Saturday night, it was

from end to end an open fair; cheap-jacks screaming; laughing crowds round them... women struggling under the weight of a baby, trying to get the Sunday dinner a little cheaper because things had begun to get stale; great louts of lads standing at the corners;... slatternly women creeping out of little public-houses.[23]

To the Mission's humble brick church of St Agatha there came in 1885 as priest-in-charge an Anglo-Irish Anglo-Catholic and Christian Socialist, the Rev. Robert Dolling. Though an extreme high churchman he was a man of very broad and liberal views, and withal one of the toughest and stoutest-hearted of mortals. Unconventional, sympathetic and tolerant, he gained extraordinary influence over all sorts and conditions of people. Campaigning against bad housing, illiteracy and drink, he kept open house for drunkards, beggars and prostitutes, and organised schools, clubs, almshouses and a gymnasium which gave local youths a much-needed outlet for their previously misdirected energies. By 1893, like Canon Jacob, he wanted a roomier and worthier church for his fast-growing congregation and by 1895 it had been built. Dolling commissioned Heywood Sumner, a friend and disciple of William Morris, to decorate the semi-dome of the now vanished lady chapel with a mosaic of the Virgin and a series of murals showing scenes from her life in sgraffito (a technique practised in Roman and Renaissance times which involves the incision of lines in coloured plaster before it has set). One of Portsmouth's major works of art, this deserved much greater appreciation than it received for a long time. But before it was finished and only five months after the new St Agatha's was consecrated Dolling fell foul of the Bishop of Winchester through his insistence on saying masses for the dead, and resigned. In ten years he had raised the roll of communicants from a dozen to 441 and collected £50,000 of which only £760 came from diocesan funds. In 1902 he died at the early age of fifty-one.[24]

Another mission, the creation of an equally remarkable though quieter personality, had begun work in Portsmouth at about the same time as that of Winchester College. Dame Agnes Weston, who has been called 'the mother of the Navy', had originally begun her welfare work for bluejackets at Devonport, where the first Sailors' Rest was opened in 1874, but now transferred her attention to the senior port. Securing a small music-hall building, she turned it into a coffee-tavern with a reading-room and other recreational facilities. Later she obtained a site in Commercial Road where with the help of generous and energetic friends she established the Royal Sailors' Rest in 1882. Additions were made to this from time to time, and in due course a second large building was erected on the site of a former public-house. Miss Weston also devoted herself with a good deal of success to alleviating the distress of the widows and orphans of sailors who had lost their lives at sea. On her death in 1918 the Admiralty accorded her the unprecedented but well-deserved honour of a naval funeral.[25]

The Boer War of 1899–1902 made on the whole less impact on Portsmouth than had the Crimean War. It was not a naval war even in part, as that had been; no great fleets went out to it, though our naval forces had presently to be prepared against possible European intervention on behalf of the Boers and two naval brigades fought on land during the early operations. One of these was partly provided from the new cruiser *Terrible*, which had been lying at Portsmouth for the previous eighteen months and now went out to the Cape under the command of the afterwards famous gunnery expert Percy Scott. The other, which suffered heavy losses in the costly victory of Graspan during the first unsuccessful attempt to relieve Ladysmith, was composed of seamen and marines from Portsmouth—the former drawn from the Naval Depot and the *Excellent*. It had been given an enthusiastic send-off by cheering crowds, as were the two regular battalions of the garrison. At the beginning of the war, too, an impromptu patriotic demonstration took place at a meeting called by the Lord Mayor in support of the Government's policy. To the accompaniment of cheers and jingoistic songs a resolution approving the war (whose seconder made the rather staggering statement that Joseph Chamberlain had combined the meekness of Moses with the patience of Job) was passed with one dissentient voice, that of a bold but luckless individual who was seized and hustled out of the hall and needed police protection to escape in safety. A relief fund was also set up for British refugees from the Transvaal and the families of servicemen killed in action.[26]

To this enthusiasm there came, here as elsewhere, a sharp shock; and after the 'Black Week' in December 1899 when three disasters within a few days showed that victory would be neither quick nor easy, detachments of the local Volunteers who had offered themselves for service in South Africa were among the reinforcements sent out, as were several scores of young Portsmouth men who had joined the regiments of Imperial Yeomanry that were being raised. Then at the end of January sympathetic crowds watched the wounded marines from Graspan, survivors of those who had carried the hill by a frontal attack at a cost of more than 50% casualties, brought back to Haslar Hospital. Later, when the tide of the war had begun to turn, the news of the relief of Mafeking in May produced an outburst of that wild excitment which gave a new word—'mafficking'—to the English language. Huge crowds marched singing and shouting up and down Commercial Road for hours, carrying soldiers and sailors shoulder-high; flags were hoisted and church bells pealed. More restrained demonstrations greeted the capture of Pretoria, the Transvaal capital, a fortnight later; but the heading in the *Hampshire Telegraph*, 'The War Nearly Over', expressed the general expectation. But instead it dragged on for two years of guerrilla warfare; and when peace was signed at last there was no more mafficking but only a subdued and relieved joy, with here and there a cheer, bells ringing and newspapers selling like wildfire. It should be added, though, that the news came on a rather wet Sunday evening and had in any case been somewhat discounted by expectation. Dolling's successor at St Agatha's, too, the Rev. Bruce Cornford, struck a dissident note by declining to observe the official day of thanksgiving for victory which followed, explaining in a letter to his parishioners that he 'had not the face to thank God that we had succeeded in taking possession of two countries which did not belong to us'.[27]

In the last quarter of the century the built-up area of the borough had nearly doubled, and by 1910 its population could no longer be contained in Portsea Island but was bursting out across Ports Creek to the mainland, so that the town was taking in the growing village of Cosham in effect if not yet in form. Ten years later formal recognition was given to this *fait accompli* by the extension of the borough limits to absorb the districts of Cosham and Paulsgrove, which had formerly been parts of the parish of Wymering.[28]

13. The two world wars: ruin and resurrection

The first world war had an impact on Portsmuthians, as on their compatriots elsewhere, which was fundamentally different from that of any previous and lesser conflict—even the Napoleonic War. Closely linked with the fighting services though the town was, its inhabitants had been mostly spectators of these earlier wars; but they, or a great many of them, were participants in this one in a variety of ways. Those Portsmuthians who were already in the Army or Navy were joined in due course by many thousands more, and some 6,000 in all gave their lives for their country. Others, many or most of them over military age, formed volunteer units for home defence or served in a volunteer ambulance brigade; while others again became munition workers or special constables, or joined the fire brigade, which was augmented in expectation of air-raids. Women took men's places in commercial establishments, banks and post offices, became tram conductors and drivers, worked in the dockyard and in munition factories, and joined the nursing services, the Waacs,* Wrens or Wrafs when these came successively into existence, or else the Women's Land Army.[1]

Several school buildings and those of various other establishments, as well as more than one private house, were converted into hospitals; as was Milton Asylum in 1918, for American troops. Food was rationed in the later part of the war, after prices had risen 91% by the beginning of 1917, owing partly to profiteering; and during the early months of 1918, when there was a serious shortage of meat, butter and other articles, people queued up, often for hours, outside the principal shops in hope of being served. Ground was taken from the public parks, Southsea Common, and even parts of Governor's Green near the Grand Parade, to be converted into allotments and cultivated by individuals for food production. Increasingly drastic restrictions were imposed on the licensing trade; licensed houses were allowed to open only between noon and 2.30 p.m. and between 6 and 9 p.m. (the previous closing-time having been 11 p.m.); orders for spirits to be consumed off the premises could be taken only on weekdays between noon and 2.30, the quantity

---

* The Women's Army Auxiliary Corps—the predecessors of the A.T.S.

must not be less than a quart, and the vessel containing it must bear a label showing where it had been obtained. The unkindest restriction, however, was that which forbade treating, though it could obviously be evaded by collusion among customers. The supply of liquor, too, was greatly reduced, so that it became common to see in the windows of public-houses such notices as 'No Beer', 'Sold Out' or 'Closed till Friday'. But one result was that drunkenness declined rapidly and during the last two years of the war it became very rare to see a drunken man in the streets.[2]

A deprivation that was felt as keenly as most, or perhaps any, was that Southsea beach and promenade were almost completely closed to the public. Except for a few score yards here and there, the whole of the sea-front was screened off by barbed wire, with a fearsome notice at each end proclaiming that sudden and violent death might befall anyone who penetrated it. The entrance to Spithead, too, was restricted to a comparatively narrow channel by a boom in the shape of a three-mile stretch of piles.[3]

Despite expectations Portsmouth enjoyed almost complete immunity from air attack. Careful precautions were taken, however, especially at night. Every alternate street-lamp was extinguished and the rest were deeply shaded in blue and green. All blinds had to be drawn half an hour after sunset, and during the four lightest months of 1918 the town authorities reverted to the practice of 100 years earlier by forbidding any street-lamps at all to be lit. As a further safeguard all church and other bells were silenced. But only once did a Zeppelin venture over the port, about eleven o'clock on the night of 25 September 1916, and then it merely dropped four bombs harmlessly into the harbour—though the German official *communiqué* announced that Portsmouth had been 'lavishly bombarded with explosive and incendiary bombs, with visible good results'.[4]

In a town whose fortunes were so closely bound up with those of the Navy, the naval reductions which followed the war were bound to have far-reaching effects. Not only was the great wartime expansion of the Senior Service rapidly reversed, but it proved impossible to maintain it even at its pre-war level, partly because of Britain's changed economic situation, and partly in consequence of the limitations imposed by the Washington Naval Treaty of 1922 with the United States, Japan, France and Italy. There was some development of Portsmouth as an experimental and training base, however. H.M.S. *Dryad*, a shore establishment in the dockyard (afterwards moved to Southwick in 1941) had already been the school for training officers specialising in navigation since 1903; in 1922 another shore establishment christened H.M.S. *Vernon* was set up as the Navy's main torpedo-training and torpedo experimental centre; and after the second world war a department of it was moved to a position between Gosport and Fareham to become a radar and electronics school under the name of H.M.S. *Collingwood*. On the other hand warship-building in the dockyard was restricted to cruisers, destroyers and submarines after 1917, and in more recent years the yard has been mainly used for reconstruction, refitting and repairs.[5]

The post-war slump in the dockyard's activities and hence its personnel naturally retarded the growth of the borough's population, though on the other hand the boundary extension of 1920 already referred to* raised it to 247,284 at the census of the following year. From this it rose only to 252,481 in the next decade and then reached a peak of about 260,000 in 1939, helped by a further eastward and westward extension of the mainland boundaries in 1932 which took in Farlington, a small part of Bedhampton and an unimportant part of Portchester; and also by the fact that the great trade depression of the early 1930s did not hit Portsmouth as badly as some other towns, thanks partly to the (still limited) rearmament program which began in 1935 and stimulated the dockyard again. On the eve of the second world war the yard, with its fifteen dry docks and its enclosed basins covering about thirty of its 300 acres, was still employing more than 15,000 men, and almost one-third of Portsmouth's 70,000 families were dependent on or connected with either it or the Navy or other Government establishments. Not only did Drayton and Farlington on the mainland therefore develop rapidly into a new major residential area, but there was also a good deal of further urban development in North End, Eastney, Milton and the district between the railway and Baffin's Pond on the eastern shore of the island. The worst of the remaining slums, too, were removed by a clearance programme which rehoused 4,700 people in 1,200 new houses and flats.

The civic authorities, moreover, had quickly decided to pursue a policy of developing Southsea's holiday resort industry as a means of countering the relative slump in the dockyard. In 1923 they therefore bought Southsea Common from the War Department, from which they had previously rented the use of it, for £45,000; bought out for another £5,000 the manorial rights of the heirs of the Leekes, which the family had retained when they sold the Common to the Government in 1785; and spent a further £60,000 on converting what had been a still not very attractive military parade ground into a pleasure garden by the sea. At the same time they launched a vigorous publicity campaign with satisfactory results[7]. The consequent further development of Southsea as a resort had a steadying influence on the city's economy, in spite of the instability of employment in the dockyard during the 1920s and 1930s. Evidence of this stabilising influence was afforded by the fact that comparatively few county borough councils at that time were levying a lower rate per head of population for public assistance.[8]

Further commercial development of the Camber was also undertaken, and the revenue from the dues charged at its docks on coal, timber,

---

* See above, p. 135.

produce from the Channel Islands and other imports was upwards of £20,000 a year by 1939;[9] while the opening in 1932 of an airport at Hilsea which at the end of the between-war period was employing nearly 2,000 people brought a new industry into the city besides promoting its general development. For some time, however, many Portsmuthians were inclined to look askance at the airport because it cost an average of £7,000 a year in rates.[10] Another and more established industry, the manufacture of corsets for which Portsmouth had long been noted—indeed it used to be said that all it produced outside the dockyard was beer and corsets—also developed; and in 1939 more than a dozen factories were emplying 2,500 women in making them. The largest of these, the Twilfit factory in Arundel Street, had 1,200 women and 200 men on its payroll.[11]

In 1926 Portsmouth formally became a city, and a year later a diocese of Portsmouth was created under Bishop Lovett. As between the churches of the two ancient parishes of the island, St Thomas's in Old Portsmouth and St Mary's in the parish of Portsea, the former had the older building and was therefore chosen to be the cathedral. It was then decided to extend it, and three stages of the proposed extensions had been completed when war broke out. The further and more revolutionary extensions which were undertaken after the war were planned as a memorial to D-Day,[12] when many thousands of British fighting-men and their allies left the shores of Portsmouth to invade the Continent under the command of Field-Marshal Montgomery, who as a brigadier had commanded the garrison before the war.

The second world war differed again vastly from the first in its impact on the people of Portsmouth. In 1914–18 many of them had gone to the war; but this time the war also came to them.

Its effect on the city was devastating, even though it had been anticipated that Portsmouth would be a major target for the enemy's bombs and more than a million pounds had been spent beforehand on civil defence preparations.[13] The first air-raid came in the early evening of 11 July 1940. The Kingston Cross district suffered, and eighteen people were killed and eighty injured. Four of the twenty-four raiding planes were brought down, and within ten days £6,000 had been subscribed to a fund started by the *Evening News* to provide a Spitfire to hit back on the city's behalf. Eventually £12,365 19s 1d was received for this purpose.

On 12 August came the second raid, which resulted in widespread damage. For twenty minutes twenty-five bombers pounded Portsea, Old Portsmouth and parts of Southsea, as well as Gosport and the Isle of Wight. In Portsmouth thirteen were killed and over 100 injured. A large fire was caused at the Harbour Railway Station, helped on by the wooden piles on which it was built out over the water. Twelve days later the third raid occurred, in which forty planes killed 125 persons, wounded 300 and rendered at least 500 homeless. Two days afterwards the raiders came again, but this time they were driven off and for once the bombs intended for the city fell harmlessly in fields at Farlington and Langstone. Then came raid after raid, in one of which the famous old George Hotel in the High Street suffered along with most of the rest of that thoroughfare and the 'Nelson Bedroom', in which the Admiral had slept when he stayed ashore in Portsmouth, was destroyed.

After 15 December the Germans gave up daylight raids because of their losses and began to come at night. The worst attack was the great fire-blitz of 10 January 1941, when 300 raiders dropped 25,000 incendiaries besides high-explosive bombs and at one time twenty-eight major fires were burning with no effective water-supply to check them, since the water-mains had been broken. There were in all 2,314 fires; 3,000 persons were left homeless, 171 killed and 430 injured. Three showers of incendiary bombs fell on the Guildhall, the third of which set the building alight, and then a high-explosive bomb hit the roof, which fell in. The Lord Mayor and A.R.P. personnel had left the building barely in time. All next day flames flared from the 200-feet-high tower, which blazed like a torch till the copper plates of the cupola fell off and the ruin was complete. Weeks passed before the burned-out interior was cool enough to be entered, revealing a scene of utter destruction. Only the outer walls remained standing. Pictures, statues, beautiful walnut panelling, mosaic paving, furniture, the valuable organ and others of the city's civic possessions were gone. The one fortunate exception was the treasure in the muniment room, where the archives and the priceless Corporation plate, including the Bodkin loving-cup dating from 1525 and the mace presented by a mayor in 1658, were found to be intact, since the muniment room was under the tower and so had escaped the worst of the heat.* The garrison church, the one-time Domus Dei, was likewise reduced to a burnt-out shell, which it still remains; the main shopping centres in Palmerston, King's and Commercial Roads were ruined; and the other buildings destroyed included six churches, a hospital and part of another, Clarence Pier, a music-hall and three cinemas, the dockyard school, a drill-hall, a hotel and the Royal Sailors' Rest.

The electricity supply had been cut off by a direct hit on the generating station; and so many restaurants were destroyed, as well as fifty food-shops (158 more of which were damaged), that emergency arrangements had to be made for feeding the population in open-air canteens. On 31 January the Prime Minister, Winston Churchill, came down to give the city the Government's congratulations and thanks for standing up so indomitably to the enemy's attacks; and on 6 February King George VI and Queen Elizabeth visited Portsmouth to bring encouragement and were given a rousing reception. 'You are a wonderful people', they said, 'and we are very proud of Portsmouth'.

---

* The Guildhall was rebuilt after the war and reopened in 1959.

On 9 March a fresh series of savage night attacks on the city and port began. The first lasted for four hours; but though it was a concentrated raid and the Germans announced that fierce fires and vast destruction had been caused, there were only six civilian casualties. When the raiders came again the next night, however, the story was different. The attack lasted six hours and the casualties were 93 killed and 250 injured, though four of the enemy were brought down. On the 11th they came once more, inflicted more damage, killed 21 persons and injured 48. April was also a month of raids, some of which lasted for most of the night, and in one of which, on the 27th, the death-roll was over 100 and the injured numbered 275.

After Hitler turned his attention to Russia things began to quieten down, as in the rest of the country; but in May 1944 Portsmouth shared in one of the belated attacks which the enemy made when they realised that the build-up for the invasion of Europe had begun. When their last efforts, the V-bombs, commenced only two of these fell within the city, the second—the last bomb to fall on Portsmouth—causing 15 deaths and 82 injuries.

In all there were sixty-seven raids on Portsmouth, three of them major attacks—those of 24 August 1940 and 10 January and 10 March 1941. The others were sometimes destructive but at other times not so heavy, many being 'hit and run' raids by small forces or lone raiders. A total of 1,320 high-explosive bombs,* approximately 38,000 incendiaries and 38 parachute mines or 'land mines' (which were the most destructive of all) were dropped on the city. 930 civilians were killed, 1,216 admitted to hospital and 1,621 less seriously injured. In relation to the number of attacks and the intensity of some of them this was a comparatively light casualty list; a fact attributed to the good protection provided by private and public shelters, the readiness of the population to avail themselves of the safety measures (here the heritage of discipline in a city so closely linked with the Services probably told) and the efficiency of the Civil Defence personnel. But the main shopping centres had been almost obliterated; the fine High Street that had been one of the prides of the old town had been shattered and half ruined; few streets in any part of the city had escaped the raiders' attentions; there was not a part of it which did not show hideous scars and in some places completely devastated areas; the Guildhall had been burnt out, the Garrison Church partly gutted, thirty other churches and mission halls destroyed or very badly damaged, and ten slightly damaged, eight schools destroyed, nine seriously damaged and eleven slightly, one hospital destroyed and another badly damaged, four cinemas and a music-hall destroyed and one damaged. In 1939 Portsmouth had contained nearly 30,000 properties, some of which had been damaged twice, thrice or even four

---

* In addition to some hundreds which fell in the sea or on the foreshore mudlands.

times, so that there had been reports of damage to over 80,000. 6,625 premises had been totally destroyed, 6,549 seriously damaged and 68,886 slightly damaged. It had become the most battered city in the country outside of London.

'Smitten city though we are', the editor of the *Evening News*, Mr William G. Easthope, nevertheless wrote in a foreword to his story of Portsmouth under the blitz, 'we are neither conquered nor dismayed. We have firmly resolved that from the ruins . . . there shall arise a new and better Portsmouth. . . . The desolation that surrounds us to-day is our grandest opportunity'. This proud boast was to be made good.

Like other British cities, Portsmouth was faced by a problem of reconstruction, the more difficult because the damage was not all concentrated in one area and materials were scarce. During the worst of the bombing the population had dropped from 260,000 to an estimated 143,000 in 1943. Then the people had begun to come back; after the war it had risen again to 244,000 and it was estimated that natural increase would bring it to 260,000 again by 1971.[14] The first and most pressing problem was to provide housing quickly, but since a lower density of rebuilding was desirable and there was a shortage of land within the city boundaries it was obviously necessary to provide accommodation for at least 40,000 people outside them. In 1944 the Corporation had therefore bought 1,672 acres of land at Leigh Park near Havant, eight miles from the city centre, where it hoped to build sufficient houses to solve the problem, in conjunction with maximum replacement within the city. Planning considerations made this project difficult, however, for it was not till 1951, after an enquiry by the Ministry of Town and Country Planning, that the Corporation was free to build as many houses there as it wished.[15] A satellite town with its own industrial estate then began to arise at Leigh Park to house the greater part of this overspill population. Nevertheless this was only the start of the solution of the overspill problem and in the subsequent years more great housing estates on the mainland, though within the city's enlarged boundaries, arose at Farlington and on the slopes of Portsdown Hill at Paulsgrove and Wymering. Then on Portsea Island itself new estates appeared at Hilsea, Stamshaw, Buckland, Burrfields, Landport and elsewhere; though on the whole more slowly, since the reconstruction of the central area had to take second place and until the middle of the 1960s many war-damaged sites remained derelict. This central reconstruction was achieved not merely by building on blitzed areas, but by the clearance of thousands of substandard houses that were still standing and the residential redevelopment of the districts concerned. Perhaps the most striking example was in the Somerstown region of east Southsea, where towering blocks of flats sprang up like a miniature Manhattan to replace the former terrace-houses.[16] However startling, and to some people aesthetically unwelcome, these blocks and the similar ones on the

Portsdown slopes may be, the local authority's solution of the problem of finding space by building high has brought sunlight and open spaces into these neighbourhoods.

Besides rehousing there was another and perhaps even greater difficulty facing a city so dependent on one main industry, and that one as closely linked with the defence services as the dockyard was. This was the renewed and still greater reduction of the Navy which followed the second world war. The first reduction, in the 1920s and early 1930s, had been met by the booming of Southsea as a holiday resort, but during and after the blitz it had of course completely ceased to function as such and the city's economy had therefore been disrupted. Without the special financial aid which Portsmouth received from the Government it would have been impossible for it to continue satisfactorily as a unit of local government at all. But this aid came to an end in 1951 and the city was left without any help from the Exchequer to meet its manifold needs.[17] It is true that Southsea soon recovered its popularity as a resort, but in view of the huge capital expenditure facing the city it could not by itself have the same steadying influence on the economy as before the war. For the moment Portsmouth seemed to have been overtaken by the march of events. A long slow decline as a city living on its memories might have lain before it.

But now began the near-miracle; not just a resurgence but a transformation, based on a determination to break out of the mould that history had imposed on it. Reaching out for a new vitality, the historic seaport set itself to attract as many new and varied light industries as possible to its area and neighbourhood. On the development and prosperity of these, and on the expansion as far as possible of the commerce of the Camber, it based its hopes for the future. An advantage of this policy was that whereas the general level of wages in the dockyard had been low the introduction of these private light manufacturing industries would offer higher wage-rates as well as more stable employment, and also more opportunities of work for women.

For these new industries land again was needed; and again, as with the rehousing problem, much of it had to be found on the mainland. This the City Council made available at Farlington, as well as smaller areas at Hilsea, Fratton and elsewhere on Portsea Island.[18] The steady build-up of industry and commerce that has followed has perhaps been Portsmouth's greatest post-war achievement. As a leading member of the City Council has written,* this diversification and expansion of industry has been so successful that the problems of the area have become its opportunities. By 1970 more than 100 new firms had established branches or in some cases their headquarters in Portsmouth and thirty existing ones had moved to fresh premises, providing in all a

---

* Councillor F. A. J. EMERY-WALLIS in *Progressive Portsmouth*, p. 3.

total of 24,000 extra jobs. They include firms concerned with plastics, engineering, computers, steel fabrication, microtools, castings, surgical products, fashion wear, packaging, office equipment, furniture, clocks, ice-cream, chemicals and much else besides.[19] To quote a *Financial Times* survey, 'the city has become one of the largest centres of employment in south-east England outside greater London and is providing one of the most varied industrial and commercial scenes to be found anywhere in Britain'.[20]

. . . 'Industrial *and* commercial', since in order to avoid creating any imbalance in the employment structure by placing too much reliance on industrial activity and also partly because of the growing scarcity of industrial land, the city is seeking to encourage greater attention to office development. Among the firms now based on Portsmouth are the Zürich Insurance Company, CJB (Products) Limited and the United Kingdom headquarters of IBM. Moreover with the building of the Albert Johnson Quay on four and a half acres of reclaimed land at Mile End in 1967, with plans in hand for the construction of a new dock as an extension to it, and a further possible extension to follow, Portsmouth is rapidly developing as a commercial port, handling over a million tons of cargo a year.[21]

To meet the growing scarcity of industrial land and also to provide more public open spaces and playing-fields land has been and is being reclaimed from the sea. In 1962–4 a half-mile-long bund was built across the entrance to Milton Lake, an arm of Langstone Harbour. The ninety acres thus enclosed were then reclaimed by tipping refuse and were afterwards laid out as an open space and playing-field area. Towards the end of the 1960s, when it again became necessary to provide new tipping space, nearly 500 acres of Portsmouth Harbour north of Horsea Island were selected for reclamation. Two chalk bunds were built and the area they enclosed is now being rapidly transformed into land which will be used mainly to provide employment and facilities for the people of the region.[22]

Land and buildings released by the Ministry of Defence have also been adapted to residential, recreational, cultural and public amenity purposes. In 1958 the Council bought the Round Tower and Point Battery and in 1960 the Square Tower; and by restoring the fortifications, extending the promenade along this section of the seafront and firmly rejecting plans which had been submitted for various forms of commercial development such as a restaurant, a hotel, a cafeteria, a sailing centre and a students' hostel created a very attractive amenity area by 1964. A similar policy was pursued after Southsea Castle and its environs had been purchased in 1959. This time the proposals included a hotel (hotly backed, a zoo, restaurant and putting-course, skating-rink, bowling alley, swimming-pool, ballrooms, jazz cellar, roadhouse, motel, congress hall, exhibition hall, marine land or oceanarium (negatived on climatic grounds), floral hall and multi-purpose sports hall. But eventually after restoration had been carried out and the line of the ramparts laid out with a public walk along the top, the Castle was converted into a museum depicting the naval and military history of Portsmouth.[23] After the Portsmouth garrison was closed in 1960 the former Clarence Barracks, too, were made into a city museum and art gallery, opened in 1972. Fort Cumberland, which is likewise no longer in military use, is now under the control of the Ministry of the Environment's Directorate of Ancient Monuments; while Lumps Fort, bought by the Corporation in 1932, was also converted into a recreation area with a rose garden which is one of the beauties of Portsmouth.[23]

A handicap which had previously imposed a constraint on any large-scale development on Portsea Island was removed when in order to overcome the deficiencies of the existing drainage system a new drainage scheme was prepared which involved the building of a new pumping station at Eastney. All the foul water in the city and most of the storm water on the island had been drained or pumped to the previous station, whose plant was either obsolete or in need of renewal, so that at times of heavy rain it could not deal with peak flows, which led to flooding of low-lying areas. The new station was completed in 1971.[24]

Though Portsmouth lacks a university, there have been striking developments in higher and further education, and the student population in its colleges increased from 3,357 in 1960 to 14,168 in 1971. It has the largest grouping of technological education south of Birmingham and west of London. There are over 5,000 full-time and part-time students in its Polytechnic (as the former Municipal and then Regional College of Technology was rechristened in 1969), though it is not yet well served for accommodation; 7,600 in Highbury Technical College which was opened in 1962; and 550 in the College of Art and Design for which a new building was completed in 1960. In addition the College of Education (the former Teachers' Training College) provides training in teaching for about 1,000 students—thrice the number that it had little more than a decade ago. A major programme of providing new and improved schools has also been undertaken since the war.[25]

Increasing emphasis, too, has been placed on the need to improve the environment, and there has been a great development of open spaces, parks and recreational facilities. The acreage of these has been more than doubled since 1950.[26]

But in spite of all changes and innovations problems remain. Two out of every five men in Portsmouth are still dependent on the defence services in one way or another for their employment. The level of unemployment, though below the national average, is usually not far short of double the average for London and the south-east, and the abler and more ambitious of the younger folk still tend to drift away. Thirty per cent of A-level holders go elsewhere for their first jobs, and many of the young who remain to work in the city go to live on the municipal estates outside or on the verge of its boundaries when they marry, thus strengthening the tendency for Portsea Island itself to have an ageing population. A survey in 1965 showed that out of 104,000 jobs in the city 83,000 were still on the island, but out of these 83,000 workers there were 31,000 who travelled from the mainland, 21,000 of them from outside the city limits. Three-quarters of them came by car or bus, which in view of the restricted road access to the island has meant wearisome journeys to work and long traffic jams at every rush hour.[27]

Until 1941 the only road connection between the island and the mainland was over Portsbridge. A scheme for a second connection by an Eastern Road leaving the mainland east-west coast road at Drayton, crossing Port Creek at its eastern end and running close to Langstone Harbour had been adopted at the end of the first world war and work begun on it, but this was stopped during the economic depression of the early 1930s, leaving the road extending northwards out of the city only as far as the airport and the municipal golf course. Resumed in 1934 with a grant from the national exchequer, it was completed in 1941. But even when thus reinforced Portsmouth's road system had become more obviously inadequate than ever twenty years later, and in 1965 the City Council accepted a plan of the City Engineer for a new road pattern. Basically this provides for two north-south routes, one on the eastern side of the island and the other on the west, linked together at the southern end by an east-west road; the whole forming a U-shaped loop crossed at its top by the new south coast trunk road (M27). An enlarged and extended Eastern Road, that is, will form a link from the M27 (now completed from the east as far as Portsbridge) to a new east-west road in the south of the island, part of which is already under construction. On the west of the city another north-south road will similarly leave the M27, cross the stretches of reclaimed land in the north of Portsmouth Harbour and travel along the island's western shore before veering into the city. The plan had also proposed an inner ring road to by-pass the Commerical Road shopping and business area north of the Guildhall, enabling this to be closed to traffic and a shopping precinct created. These parts of the plan have already been carried into effect.[28]

Linked to these projects and achievements is the most eye-catching and exciting change of all—the new city centre which is being created in the area around the restored Guildhall. In 1963 the Council chose Lord Esher to prepare an overall plan and act as co-ordinating architect for this area. After a public enquiry had resulted in the approval of the plan the demolition of old buildings cleared the way for the marriage of the new road-pattern with a new and extensive traffic-free Guildhall Square where additional premises for the Polytechnic, blocks of offices and shops, a civic office block and a new central library and arts centre are now arising or will shortly arise.[29]

Portsmouth's situation at the moment is somewhat complicated, however, by the fact that the recent reorganisation of local government areas has coincided with a period when the face of the city is changing substantially. On 1 April 1974 it embarked on a new phase in its long history and, though retaining its status as a city, became also a district within the county. The former City Council duly handed over its assets and its obligations, its programmes and its plans, partly to the new County Council, partly to the new District Council, partly to the Area Health Authority and partly to the new Water Authority. But as the last Lord Mayor of the old dispensation, Councillor J. P. N. Brogden, said in his inaugural speech, Portsmouth 'shares a determination to make the new system a strong and cohesive one [by having] strong links with the county and with its neighbouring authorities'. It has entered this new era with a clear picture of its future policies and programmes—the best means of ensuring that its development will not be cramped and that its present rate of progress and improvement will be maintained.

Notes

ABBREVIATIONS USED

DNB	Dictionary of National Biography
GATES	W. GATES, *History of Portsmouth*
GATES, *Records*	W. GATES, *Records of the Portsmouth Corporation, 1835–1927.*
LIPSCOMB	CAPT. F. W. LIPSCOMB, R.N., *Heritage of Sea-Power.*
LLOYD	N. PEVSNER and D. LLOYD, *The Buildings of England: Hampshire and the Isle of Wight.*
THOMAS	G. THOMAS, *Historical Geography of Portsmouth and Gosport.*
V.C.H. Hants.	*Victoria History of the Counties of England: Hampshire.*
WHITE	W. WHITE, *History, Gazeteer and Directory of Hampshire and the Isle of Wight.*

CHAPTER I: THE FIRST 'OLD PORTSMOUTH': PORTCHESTER

1. Where no other source is specifically stated, this chapter is based on Professor BARRY CUNLIFFE's *Portsmouth Paper* No. 1, on Portchester Castle.
2. R. G. COLLINGWOOD AND SIR J. N. L. MYRES, *Roman Britain and the English Settlements*, p. 398.
3. SIR F. STENTON, *Anglo-Saxon England*, p. 20n.
4. *Ibid.*, p. 262. CUNLIFFE, B., *Interim Report on Excavations at Portchester Castle, 1969–71*, p. 83.

CHAPTER II: PORTSMOUTH IN THE MIDDLE AGES

1. *V.C.H. Hants.*, III, p. 172.
2. *Ibid.*
3. R. HUBBOCK, *Portsea Island Churches (Portsmouth Paper* No. 5), p. 3. GATES, p. 43.
4. *Ibid.*, p. 32. HUBBOCK, *op. cit.*, p. 4.
5. *V.C.H. Hants.*, III, pp. 173–4 and 176. GATES, pp. 66–7. LIPSCOMB, pp. 20–1.
6. *V.C.H. Hants.*, III, p. 174.
7. LIPSCOMB, pp. 22–3.
8. *Ibid.*, pp. 23–4. *V.C.H.Hants.*, V, p. 361. GATES, pp. 70–1.

9. *Ibid.*, pp. 77–80. *V.C.H.Hants.*, pp. 206–8. HUBBOCK, *op. cit.*, pp. 3–4, 8–9, 11. LIPSCOMB, pp. 31–2.
10. *Ibid.*, pp. 29–30.
11. *V.C.H.Hants.*, V, p. 362. LIPSCOMB. p. 32.
12. *V.C.H.Hants.*, III, p. 174.
13. *Ibid.*, pp. 175, 185 and n., 293. C. PLATT, *Medieval Southampton*, p. 15.
14. *V.C.H.Hants.*, III, pp. 177–180.
15. *Ibid.*, pp. 180–1.
16. *Ibid.*, p. 183.
17. *Ibid.*, p. 182.
18. *Ibid.*, p. 184.
19. H. J. SPARKS, *The Story of Portsmouth*, p. 111.
20. *V.C.H.Hants.*, III, p. 184.
21. *Ibid.*, pp. 184–5.
22. *Ibid.*, p. 174.
23. Quoted in LIPSCOMB, p. 32.
24. PLATT, *op. cit.*, p. 38.
25. *Ibid.*, p. 119.
26. *V.C.H.Hants.*, V, pp. 363–6. LIPSCOMB, p. 34.
27. *Ibid.*, p. 35. *V.C.H.Hants.*, V, pp. 364–5.
28. *Ibid.*, pp. 365–6.
29. *Ibid.*, p. 367.
30. N. PEVSNER AND D. LLOYD, *The Buildings of England and the Isle of Wight*, p. 390.
31. A. TEMPLE PATTERSON, *Southampton*, pp. 30–1.
32. LIPSCOMB, pp. 38–9.
33. *V.C.H.Hants.*, V, p. 369.
34. GATES, pp. 119–124. HUBBOCK, *op. cit.*, p. 4. LIPSCOMB, pp. 39–40 and 45.

CHAPTER III: TUDOR PORTSMOUTH: PROGRESS AND SETBACK

1. A. BALFOUR, *Portsmouth*, p. 15. LIPSCOMB, pp. 42 and 74.
2. *V.C.H.Hants.*, V, pp. 370–1. THOMAS, p. 8. LIPSCOMB, pp. 42–4.
3. *V.C.H.Hants.*, V, pp. 370–1.
4. *Ibid.*, p. 372.
5. *Ibid.* THOMAS, p. 8. LIPSCOMB, pp. 45, 49, 51–3. GATES, pp. 72–6 and 111–13.
6. THOMAS, pp. 9–11. LIPSCOMB, p. 44.
7. L. TOULMIN SMITH, (ed.), *Itinerary of John Leland, 1535–43*, pp. 282–4.
8. A. CORNEY, *Fortifications in Old Portsmouth*, pp. 33–4. MRS W. J. GUY, *Historic Portsmouth*, p. 24.
9. GATES, pp. 147–8.
10. LIPSCOMB, p. 62.
11. *Ibid.*, pp. 54–6. GATES, pp. 161–6. *V.C.H.Hants.*, V, pp. 373–4.
12. *Ibid.*, p. 375.
13. LIPSCOMB, pp. 60–1.
14. *Gentleman's Magazine*, LXII, p. 704.

15. *V.C.H.Hants.*, V. p. 375.
16. *Ibid.*
17. LIPSCOMB, pp. 73–4.
18. *Ibid.*, p. 74. THOMAS, p. 12.
19. CORNEY, *op. cit.*, p. 24.
20. THOMAS, p. 12.
21. *Ibid.*, p. 15.
22. *V.C.H.Hants.*, V, p. 376.
23. *Ibid.*, pp. 377–8.
24. GATES, pp. 179–181. LIPSCOMB, pp. 71–3.
25. *V.C.H.Hants.*, V, p. 376.
26. *Ibid.*, III, pp. 176–7. LIPSCOMB, p. 79.
27. *Ibid.*, p. 189. GATES, pp. 182–4.
28. *V.C.H.Hants.*, III, pp. 168–9 and 184.

CHAPTER IV: FOR KING OR PARLIAMENT,
1603–1660

1. THOMAS, pp. 14–17.
2. *Ibid.*, p. 15.
3. GATES, pp. 218–20
4. Where not otherwise stated, the account of the connection of the Duke of Buckingham and Captain John Mason with Portsmouth which follows is based—except for the general historical background—mainly on MISS DOROTHY DYMOND's *Portsmouth Paper* No. 17 on 'Captain John Mason and the Duke of Buckingham', to which this author is greatly indebted. Also A. TEMPLE PATTERSON, 'Great Days in Portsmouth's History' in *Portsmouth* (National Union of Teachers Conference Souvenir, 1937), pp. 10–12.
5. Camden Miscellany, XVI, *Relation of a Short Survey of the Western Counties in 1635* (ed. L. G. Wickham Legg).
6. J. WEBB, *The Siege of Portsmouth in the Civil War* (*Portsmouth Paper* No. 7). LIPSCOMB, pp. 94–101.
7. *V.C.H.Hants.*, III, p. 190; and V, p. 380.
8. *Ibid.*, V, pp. 380–1. THOMAS, p. 17. LIPSCOMB, pp. 101–4.
9. *Ibid.*, p. 105. *V.C.H.Hants.*, V, p. 382.
10. *Ibid.*, pp. 381–3. THOMAS, pp. 19–21. LIPSCOMB, pp. 106–7.
11. The account of Hesilrige's bid for control which follows is based on MISS DOROTHY DYMOND's 'Portsmouth and the Fall of the Puritan Republic' (*Portsmouth Paper* No. 11), to which this author is greatly indebted.

CHAPTER V: THE RISE TO PRIMACY AS A
NAVAL PORT

1. S. PEPYS, *Diary*, pp. 83 and 113.
2. *V.C.H.Hants.*, V, p. 384. THOMAS, pp. 23 and 28. LIPSCOMB, p. 123. V. BONHAM-CARTER, *In a Liberal Tradition*, pp. 7–9.
3. GATES, pp. 286–90. LIPSCOMB, pp. 124–5.
4. CORNEY, *op. cit.*, pp. 8–10 and 25–6. LLOYD, *op. cit.*, p. 419.
5. CORNEY, *op. cit.*, p. 25. GATES, pp. 213–17. THOMAS, p. 30.

6. *Ibid.*, pp. 29–31.
7. LIPSCOMB, pp. 133–5.
8. THOMAS, pp. 24–5.
9. *Ibid.*, pp. 31 and 37. *V.C.H.Hants.*, V, p. 386.
10. THOMAS, p. 30.
11. *Ibid.*, pp. 32–3.
12. GATES, pp. 348–52. LIPSCOMB, p. 139. GUY, *op. cit.*, p. 4.
13. BONHAM-CARTER, *op. cit.*, p. 9.

CHAPTER VI: PROGRESS AND PERIL

1. The account of the invasion threat to Portsmouth which follows is an abridgement of that contained in PATTERSON, *The Other Armada*.
2. G. LACOUR-GAYET, *La marine militaire de la France sous le règne de Louis XV*, pp. 231–2. C. C. LLOYD, *The Nation and the Navy*, p. 122.
3. *The Portsmouth Guide*, 1775, p. 23. *V.C.H.Hants.*, V, pp. 390 and 395. THOMAS, pp. 38–9.
4. *Ibid.*, p. 38.
5. GATES, pp. 455–9. LIPSCOMB, pp. 155–7. *V.C.H.Hants.*, V, p. 393.
6. DNB, arts. on Samuel Bentham and M. I. Brunel. THOMAS, p. 42. BALFOUR, *op. cit.*, p. 6.
7. ANON., *Journal of a Tour to the Western Counties of England performed in 1807*.
8. THOMAS, pp. 46–7.
9. *Ibid.*, p. 59. LLOYD, p. 421. *The Portsmouth Guide*, 1775, p. 39.
10. *V.C.H.Hants.*, III, p. 191. THOMAS, p. 65.
11. GATES, pp. 148–150.
12. *Ibid.*, p. 369.
13. M. LEWIS, *Social History of the British Navy, 1793–1815*, pp. 143–5.
14. H. SARGEANT, *History of Portsmouth Theatres* (*Portsmouth Paper No. 13*), pp. 3–11.
15. LLOYD, p. 456. BALFOUR, *op. cit.*, pp. 24–5. GATES, pp. 583–4.
16. WHITE, p. 276.
17. *Ibid.*
18. THOMAS, pp. 60–1. CORNEY, *op. cit.*, p. 12. LLOYD, pp. 419–20. A. D. SAUNDERS, *Hampshire Coastal Defence since the Introduction of Artillery*, p. 148.
19. THOMAS, p. 67.
20. R. S. HORNE, *The Church of St. Ann in H.M. Dockyard at Portsmouth*, pp. 1–4. HUBBOCK, *op. cit.*, p. 6.
21. THOMAS, p. 21.
22. W. D. COOPER, *Methodism in Portsmouth, 1750–1932* (*Portsmouth Paper No. 18*), pp. 3–4.
23. DNB, art. on Hanway.
24. *John Pounds Centenary Biography* (unpaginated pamphlet published at Portsmouth, 1939).

CHAPTER VII: TOWN GOVERNMENT AND LOCAL POLITICS IN THE EIGHTEENTH CENTURY

1. *V.C.H.Hants.*, III, p. 177. *Report on Municipal Corporations*, 1835, pp. 803 and 811. BONHAM-CARTER, *op. cit.*, p. 15.

2. Improvement Acts and Proceedings of Commissioners in Portsmouth City Record Office.
3. J. CRAMER, *History of the Police of Portsmouth* (*Portsmouth Paper* No. 2), pp. 3–10.
4. MISS M. HALLETT, *Portsmouth's Water Supply* (*Portsmouth Paper* No. 12), pp. 3–4.
5. D. DEFOE, *Journal of a Tour through England and Wales* (Everyman), p. 138.
6. BONHAM-CARTER, *op. cit.*, p. 14.
7. *Ibid.*, pp. 6 and 10–22. A. GEDDES, *Portsmouth during the Great French Wars, 1770–1800* (*Portsmouth Paper* No. 9), pp. 3–10.

CHAPTER VIII: THE GREAT FRENCH WARS,
1793–1815

1. GUY, *op. cit.*, pp. 5–6. WHITE, p. 253.
2. Quoted in GATES, pp. 486–8.
3. *Ibid.*, pp. 487 and 491.
4. ANON., *Journal of a Tour*...
5. *Ibid.*
6. GATES, pp. 553–4. LIPSCOMB, pp. 175–6.
7. GATES, pp. 565–70.
8. GEDDES, *op. cit.*, p. 17.
9. *Ibid.*, pp. 17–19. E. P. THOMPSON, *The Making of the English Working Class*, pp. 147–8.
10. Quoted in GEDDES, *op. cit.*, p. 20.
11. *Ibid.*
12. *Ibid.*, pp. 20–1.
13. *Ibid.*, p. 21.
14. Except where otherwise stated, the account of this which follows is an abridgement of PATTERSON, *The Naval Mutiny at Spithead, 1797* (*Portsmouth Paper* No. 5).
15. GEDDES, *op. cit.*, pp. 4–9.

CHAPTER IX: 'PEACE, RETRENCHMENT AND
REFORM', 1815–35

1. WHITE, p. 247. THOMAS, p. 100.
2. *Ibid.*, p. 75.
3. GATES, p. 606.
4. *Ibid.*, pp. 606–8.
5. COBBETT, *Rural Rides*, 4 Dec. 1821.
6. WHITE, p. 247. THOMAS, p. 114.
7. COBBETT, *op. cit.*, 19 Nov. 1822.
8. C. HADFIELD, *The Canals of Southern England*, pp. 97–8.
9. *Ibid.*, pp. 117–123 and 272–3.
10. THOMAS, p. 100.
11. WHITE, p. 260. GATES, p. 284.
12. Except where otherwise stated the account of the early development of Southsea which follows is based on R. C. RILEY, *The Growth of*

Southsea as a Naval Satellite and Victorian Resort (*Portsmouth Paper* No. 16).

13. GUY, *op. cit.*, p. 5.
14. *John Pounds Centenary Biography.*
15. *Report on the Municipal Corporations*, pp. 804–7.
16. *Ibid.*, p. 807.
17. A. TEMPLE PATTERSON, *Radical Leicester*, pp. 199–204.
18. *Report on Municipal Corporations*, pp. 807–8 and 817.
19. *Ibid.*, p. 807.
20. BONHAM-CARTER, *op. cit.*, pp. 31–4 and 44–71. GATES, *Records*, p. 266.
21. *Report on Municipal Corporations*, p. 810.
22. BONHAM-CARTER, *op. cit.*, p. 68.

CHAPTER X: EXPANSION RESUMED, 1835–60

1. *Report on Municipal Corporations*, p. 801.
2. GATES, *Records*, pp. 11–12.
3. CRAMER, *op. cit.*, pp. 11–12.
4. GATES, *Records*, pp. 15 and 17. WHITE, pp. 262–3.
5. *Ibid.*, p. 247. THOMAS, p. 114.
6. *Ibid.*, p. 104. WHITE, p. 255.
7. *Ibid.*, p. 267. GATES, *Records*, p. 28.
8. *Ibid.*, p. 18. WHITE, pp. 265–6.
9. *Ibid.*, p. 266. GATES, *Records*, p. 33.
10. WHITE, p. 266. E. COURSE, *Portsmouth Railways* (*Portsmouth Paper* No. 6), p. 16.
11. GATES, *Records*, p. 28.
12. COURSE, *op. cit.*, pp. 3–4.
13. GATES, pp. 469–73; and *Records*, pp. 30–1. WHITE, p. 267.
14. COURSE, *op. cit.*, pp. 5–8.
15. THOMAS, pp. 114–6.
16. RILEY, *op. cit.*, pp. 6–12.
17. MRS M. J. HOAD, *Portsmouth as Others Have Seen It, 1790–1900* (*Portsmouth Paper* No. 20), pp. 11–12.
18. WHITE, p. 260.
19. S. M. ELLIS, *George Meredith*, pp. 31–2.
20. SARGEANT, *op. cit.*, pp. 20–2.
21. WHITE, p. 257.
22. SIR W. BESANT, *Autobiography*, pp. 7–8.
23. ELLIS, *op. cit.*, pp. 35–6.
24. BESANT, *op. cit.*, pp. 9–13.
25. *Ibid.*, pp. 19–23.
26. J. NOON, *King Cholera Comes to Portsmouth*, pp. 9–12.
27. *Ibid.*, p. 8.
28. GATES, *Records*, pp. 52–3.
29. WHITE, p. 263.
30. *Ibid.*, p. 265. GATES, pp. 68–9.
31. HALLETT, *op. cit.*, pp. 5–20.
32. *Ibid.*, p. 22.
33. *Ibid.*

34. R. RAWLINSON, *Report to the General Board of Health on a Preliminary Enquiry into the. . . Sanitary Condition of. . . the Borough of Portsmouth*, pp. 86–7.
35. HALLETT, *op. cit.*, p. 23.
36. NOON, *op. cit.*, p. 3. GATES, *Records*, p. 52.
37. HALLETT, *op cit.*, pp. 33–4.
38. *Ibid.*, p. 24.
39. GATES, *Records*, pp. 80, 97–8, 122.
40. WHITE, p. 264.
41. *Ibid.*, p. 266.
42. *Ibid.*, pp. 267–74.
43. *Ibid.*, p. 274.
44. *Ibid.*, pp. 275–6.
45. SARGEANT, *op. cit.*, pp. 11–17.

CHAPTER XI: MID-VICTORIAN PORTSMOUTH
WARS AND RUMOURS OF WAR

1. The first three paragraphs of this chapter are an abridgement of HOAD AND PATTERSON, *Portsmouth and the Crimean War* (*Portsmouth Paper* No. 19).
2. *Hampshire Telegraph*, 4, 11 and 18 Mar; 8 and 29 April; and 6 May 1854.
3. *Ibid.*, 3, 10 and 17 Feb., 1855; 30 April 1856.
4. Except where otherwise stated, the account of the circumstances leading to the building of the Portsdown and Spithead forts which follows is an abridgement of PATTERSON, '*Palmerston's Folly*': *the Portsdown and Spithead Forts* (*Portsmouth Paper* No. 3).
5. LLOYD, pp. 421 and 428.
6. GATES, pp. 503–9. *Hampshire Telegraph*, 21 May, 20 Oct., 5 and 26 Nov. 1859; 25 Feb., 10 and 24 Mar. and 7 April 1860.
7. *Ibid.*, 4 and 25 Aug. and 15 Dec. 1860; 16 Feb. and 3 Mar. 1861; 6 Dec. 1862. GATES, pp. 503–4.
8. LLOYD, pp. 410, 417, 422 and 451.
9. BALFOUR, *op. cit.*, p. 55. GUY, *op. cit.*, p. 17.

CHAPTER XII: STEADY ADVANCE, 1860–1914

1. WHITE, p. 247. THOMAS, pp. 138–140. LLOYD, p. 451.
2. *Kelly's Directory of Hampshire* for 1867, 1875, 1885 and 1895.
3. LLOYD, pp. 390 and 445. THOMAS, p. 140.
4. RILEY, *op. cit.*, pp. 12–16.
5. GUY, *op. cit.*, p. 23.
6. RILEY, *op. cit.*, pp. 16–24.
7. COURSE, *op. cit.*, pp. 17–21.
8. GATES, *Records*, pp. 93 and 113. THOMAS, pp. 128–31 and 145.
9. *Ibid.*, pp. 146–7 and 170–2.
10. GATES, *Records*, pp. 184 and 216. *Kelly's Directory of Portsmouth*, 1903, 1915 and 1922.
11. LLOYD, pp. 428–9. GATES, *Records*, p. 232.

12. *Ibid.*, p. 140.
13. *Ibid.*, pp. 227 and 230.
14. *Ibid.*, p. 139. LLOYD, pp. 448–9. BALFOUR, *op. cit.*, p. 50.
15. GATES, *Records*, p. 174.
16. RILEY, *op. cit.*, p. 20.
17. GATES, *Records*. p. 239.
18. *Kelly's Directories of Portsmouth and Hampshire.*
19. HUBBOCK, *op. cit.*, pp. 10 and 15–16.
20. R. R. DOLLING, *Ten Years in a Portsmouth Slum*, p. 9.
21. D. GULLIVER, *Dame Agnes Weston*, pp. 54–5.
22. O. E. OSBORNE, *The Life of Father Dolling*, p. 68.
23. DOLLING, *op. cit.*, p. 11.
24. *Ibid.*, *passim.* HUBBOCK, *op. cit.*, p. 16.
25. DAME AGNES WESTON, *My Life among the Bluejackets*, *passim.* GULLIVER, *op. cit.*, *passim.*
26. *Hampshire Telegraph*, 9 Sept., 21 Oct. and 4 Nov. 1899.
27. *Ibid.*, 13 Jan., 2 Feb., 26 May, 2 and 9 June 1900; 7 June 1902.
28. THOMAS, p. 168. GATES, *Records*, p. 280.

CHAPTER XIII: THE TWO WORLD WARS: RUIN AND RESURRECTION

1. GATES (ed.), *Portsmouth and the Great War*, pp. 21–66.
2. *Ibid.*, pp. 88–90, 94–7 and 122–3.
3. *Ibid.*, p. 70.
4. *Ibid.*
5. THOMAS, pp. 172, 204 and 210.
6. *Ibid.*, p. 211. *Picture Post*, 19 Aug. 1939. Art. on 'Portsmouth: Post-War Recovery and Progress' in *Municipal Journal*, 1 July 1955, p. 1747. *Kelly's Directory*, 1933 and 1935.
7. *Picture Post*, 19 Aug. 1939.
8. Art. in *Municipal Journal*, 1 July 1955, p. 1742.
9. GUY, *op. cit.*, p. 30. *Picture Post*, 19 Aug. 1939.
10. *Ibid.*
11. *Ibid.*
12. GUY, *op. cit.*, p. 34. HUBBOCK, *op. cit.*, pp. 18–21. V. BLANCHARD (ed.), *Records of Portsmouth Corporation, 1956–65*, pp. 176–7.
13. The account of Portsmouth under the blitz which follows is based on the booklet *Smitten City: the story of Portsmouth in the Air Raids, 1940–44*, published by the *Evening News*.
14. Art. in *Municipal Journal*, 1 July 1955, pp. 1741 and 1748. The population in 1971 was in fact 197,431.
15. *Ibid.*, pp. 1741 and 1748.
16. *Times* Supplement on Portsmouth, 3 Mar. 1970.
17. Art. in *Municipal Journal*, 1 July 1955, p. 1742.
18. *Ibid.*, p. 1749.
19. *Times* Supplement, 3 Mar, 1970. *Progress in Portsmouth*, p. 4.
20. Quoted in *ibid.*, p. 4.
21. *Ibid.*, p. 3. *Times* Supplement, 3 Mar. 1970. *Note on Local Government Services, 1960–72*, pp. 8–9 and 19.
22. *Ibid.*, p. 13.

23. *Ibid.*, p. 19. BLANCHARD, *op. cit.*, pp. 38, 94–5 and 102.
24. *Note on Local Government Services*, pp. 12–13. Art. in *Municipal Journal*, 1 July 1955, p. 1767.
25. *Note on Local Government Services*, pp. 9–10.
26. *Ibid.*, p. 15.
27. *Times* Supplement, 3 Mar. 1970.
28. *Ibid. Note on Local Government Services*, pp. 10–11. Art. in *Municipal Journal*, 1 July 1955, p. 1771.
29. *Progress in Portsmouth*, p. 12.

Bibliography

ANON.: *Journal of a Tour to the Western Counties of England performed in 1807* (London, 1809).

BALFOUR, A.: *Portsmouth* (in City Buildings Series, London, 1970).

BESANT, SIR W.: *Autobiography* (London, 1902).

BESANT, SIR W. and J. RICE: *By Celia's Arbour* (London, 1878).

BLANCHARD, V. (ed.): *Records of the Portsmouth Corporation, 1936–45* (Portsmouth, 1946).

BLANCHARD, V. and BARNETT, G. E. (ed.): *Records of the Portsmouth Corporation, 1946–55* (Portsmouth, 1956).

BLANCHARD, V. (ed.): *Records of the Portsmouth Corporation, 1956–65* (Portsmouth, 1966).

BONHAM-CARTER, V.: *In a Liberal Tradition* (London, 1960).

Camden Miscellany, Vol. XVI.

COBBETT, W.: *Rural Rides* (Reeves and Turner, London, 1893).

COLLINGWOOD, R. G., and MYRES, SIR J. N. L.: *Roman Britain and the English Settlements* (Oxford, 1936).

CORNEY, A.: *Fortifications in Old Portsmouth* (Portsmouth, 1965).

CUNLIFFE, B.: *Excavations at Portchester Castle, Hants., 1969–71*; in *The Antiquaries' Journal*, Vol. LII.

DEFOE, D.: *Journal of a Tour through England and Wales* (Everyman, London, 1928).

Dictionary of National Biography, arts. on Samuel Bentham, Marc Isambard Brunel and Jonas Hanway.

DOLLING, R. R.: *Ten Years in a Portsmouth Slum* (London, 1903).

EAST, R.: *Extracts from the Portsmouth Records* (Portsmouth, 1891).

ELLIS, S. M.: *Life of George Meredith* (London, 1919).

GATES, W.: *History of Portsmouth* (Portsmouth, 1900).

GATES, W. (ed.): *Portsmouth and the Great War* (Portsmouth, 1919).

GATES, W. (ed.): *Extracts from the Records of the Portsmouth Corporation, 1835–1927* (Portsmouth, 1928).

GATES, W. (ed.): *Extracts from the Records of the Portsmouth Corporation, 1928–30* (Portsmouth, 1931).

GATES, W. (ed.): *Extracts from the Records of the Portsmouth Corporation, 1931–5* (Portsmouth, 1936).

Gentlemen's Magazine, Vol. LXII (1792).

Guides to Portsmouth, 1775, 1800, 1802, 1823, 1828, 1835, 1837, 1839, 1840, 1841, 1843, 1847, 1849, 1850, 1852, 1859, 1860, 1877, 1889, 1893, 1896–7, 1902, 1903, 1907, 1908, 1910, 1911, 1912, 1913.

GULLIVER, MRS D.: *Dame Agnes Weston* (London and Chichester, 1971).

GUY, MRS W. J.: *Historic Portsmouth* (Portsmouth, 1968).

HADFIELD, C.: *The Canals of Southern England* (London, 1955).

Hampshire Telegraph, 1854–6, 1859–62, 1899–1902.

HORNE, R. S.: *The Church of St Ann in H.M. Dockyard at Portsmouth* (Portsmouth, 1966).

Improvement Acts; Portsmouth, 1776, 1839; Portsea, 1792.

JAYNE, R. E.: *The Story of John Pounds* (London, 1955).

Kelly's Directories of Hampshire and Portsmouth for 1861, 1875, 1887, 1895, 1903, 1915, 1923, 1935.

LACOUR-GAYET, C.: *La marine militaire de la France sous le règne de Louis XVI* (Paris, 1905).

LEWIS, M.: *Social History of the British Navy, 1793–1815* (London, 1960).

LIPSCOMB, CAPT. F. W., R.N.: *Heritage of Sea-Power* (London, 1967).

LLOYD, C. C.: *The Nation and the Navy* (London, 1954).

LLOYD, D.: section on Portsmouth in N. Pevsner and D. Lloyd, *The Buildings of England: Hampshire and the Isle of Wight* (Harmondsworth, 1967).

Municipal Journal, 1 July 1955: art. on 'Portsmouth: Post-War Recovery and Progress'.

NOON, J.: *King Cholera comes to Portsmouth* (Portsmouth, 1972).

Note on Local Government Services (Town Clerk's Department, Portsmouth, 1972).

OSBORNE, O. E.: *Life of Father Dolling* (London, 1903).

PATTERSON, A. TEMPLE: *Radical Leicester* (Leicester, 1954).

PATTERSON, A. TEMPLE: *The Other Armada* (Manchester, 1960).

PATTERSON, A. TEMPLE: *Southampton* (London, 1970).

PEPYS, S.: *Diary* (Dent's Everyman Edition, London, 1963).

Picture Post, 19 Aug. 1939: art. on Portsmouth.

PLATT, C.: *Medieval Southampton* (London, 1973).

Portsmouth (National Union of Teachers Conference Souvenir, 1937: London, 1937).

Portsmouth Papers, The (Portsmouth, 1967–73).

No. 1 CUNLIFFE, B.: *Portchester*.

2 CRAMER, J.: *History of the Police of Portsmouth*.

3 PATTERSON, A. T.: *'Palmerston's Folly': The Portsdown and Spithead Forts*.

5 PATTERSON, A. T.: *The Naval Mutiny at Spithead, 1977*.

6 COURSE, E.: *Portsmouth Railways*.

7 WEBB, J.: *The Siege of Portsmouth in the Civil War*.

8 HUBBOCK, R.: *Portsea Island Churches*.

9 GEDDES, A.: *Portsmouth during the Great French Wars*.

11 DYMOND, MISS D.: *Portsmouth and the Fall of the Puritan Republic*.

12 HALLETT, MISS M.: *Portsmouth's Water Supply, 1800–1860*.

13 SARGEANT, H.: *A History of Portsmouth Theatres*.

15 HOAD, MRS M. J., *Portsmouth as others have seen it, 1540–1790*.

16 RILEY, R. C.: *The Growth of Southsea as a Naval Satellite and Victorian Resort*.

17 DYMOND, MISS D.: *Captain John Mason and the Duke of Buckingham.*

18 COOPER, W. D.: *Methodism in Portsmouth, 1750–1932.*

19 HOAD, MRS M. J. and PATTERSON, A. T., *Portsmouth and the Crimean War.*

20 HOAD, MRS M. J.: *Portsmouth as others have seen it, 1790–1900.*

Progress in Portsmouth (Portsmouth Corporation, 1973).

RAWLINSON, R.: *Report to the General Board of Health on. . . the Sanitary Condition of. . . Portsmouth,* 1850.

Report of the Royal Commission on the Municipal Corporations, 1835.

SAUNDERS, A. D.: art. on 'Hampshire Coastal Defence since the Introduction of Artillery', in *Archaeological Journal,* Vol. CXXIII.

SAUNDERS, W. H.: *Annals of Portsmouth* (London, 1880).

SLIGHT, H. and J.: *Chronicles of Portsmouth* (London, 1828).

'Smitten City: The Story of Portsmouth in the Air Raids, 1940–44' (published by the *Portsmouth Evening News,* 1945).

SPARKS, H. J.: *The Story of Portsmouth* (Portsmouth, 1921).

STENTON, SIR F. M.: *Anglo-Saxon England* (Oxford, 1943).

THOMAS, G.: unpublished thesis on 'The Historical Geography of Portsmouth and Gosport', in the Library of the London School of Economics.

THOMPSON, E. P.: *The Making of the English Working Class* (London, 1963).

Times supplement on Portsmouth, 3 March 1970.

TOULMIN SMITH, L. (ed.): *Itinerary of John Leland, 1535–34* (London, 1964).

Victoria County History of Hampshire, Vols. III and V (London, 1908 and 1912).

WASHINGTON, E. S.: *Portsmouth in the Age of Elizabeth* (Portsmouth, 1972).

WESTON, DAME A.: *My Life among the Bluejackets* (London, 1909).

WHITE, W.: *History, Gazeteer and Directory of Hampshire,* 1859 and 1878 (London).

WICKHAM LEGG, L. G. (ed.): *Relation of a Short Survey of the Western Counties in 1635,* in *Camden Miscellany,* Vol. XVI.

Index